Best Hikes of the MARBLE
Mountain and Russian Wilderness Areas, California

16 selected trails, 137 destinations
and 93 trout fishing lakes

Art Bernstein

Mountain N' Air Books
La Crescenta, CA 91224

Best Hikes of the Marble Mountain
and Russian Wilderness Areas, California

Published in the United States of America by
Mountain N'Air Books—P.O. Box 12540, La Crescenta, CA 91224
Phones: (818) 951-4150, or (800) 446-9696; Fax: (818)951-4153

Cover photo by Art Brenstein.
Cover design by Gilberto d'Urso
Book design and maps layout by Naomi Blackburn

ISBN: 1-879415-18-6

Best Hikes Of
THE MARBLE MOUNTAIN
and Russian Wilderness Areas
California

Table of Contents:

The Marble Rim, from the Marble Gap Trail (Chapter 3)

BEST HIKES OF THE
MARBLE MOUNTAIN
and Russian Wilderness Areas, California

Sky-High Lake (Chapter 3)

INTRODUCTION

My crush on the Marble Mountains

In 1970, when my wife and I decided the Midwest didn't quite suit our needs, we ended up in a rough and tumble California cowboy town with the curious name of "Yreka." She found a job in an attorney's office and I went to work for the State Fish and Game Department. My young spouse, fresh from the asphalt hinterlands of Detroit, was amazed when her first cases involved claim jumping on gold mines.

To a young naturalist like myself, newly graduated from the University of Michigan Forestry School, Yreka proved one of the most fascinating places imaginable. Within an hour of town, one could visit Oregon, Mount Shasta and the Klamath and Salmon River canyons; explore lava formations, marble caverns and desert; and hike to over 200 high mountain lakes in two of the nation's largest Wilderness Areas.

I'd heard of the larger Wilderness, the Trinity Alps, back in Forestry School. I had not heard of the Marble Mountains, an immense, gaping square covering much of the outback between Yreka and the Pacific Coast. The Marble Mountain Wilderness, I later learned, is the fourth largest in California, a state known for sprawling, high mountain back country. The nearby Trinity Alps Wilderness is third largest in the entire American Wilderness system.

Before getting to my early experiences in the Marble Mountains, I should enlighten you on two bits of trivia involving the name

"Yreka." First, it's the Shasta Indian name for Mount Shasta. Second, "Yreka Bakery" is spelled the same backwards and forwards. The best I could come up with for my hometown of Detroit, along those lines, requires omitting the "i" to get, "Detrot's id distorted." Too bad I'm not from Dallas. Or Dalas.

Anyhow, as a fresh Fish and Game employee, I was treated to a comprehensive indoctrination in backwoods lore. It was my job to explore Wilderness creeks and hike to remote mountain lakes to see which ones had fish. Some job. At the time, I not only didn't fish, I'd never touched a live fish.

I learned quickly and it wasn't long before even Yreka felt too citified. So we moved 18 miles away, to a town called Etna, in a place called Scott Valley. The address of our tiny rented house, across from the rodeo grounds, was #1 Main Street. From our front porch, the high peaks of what is now the Russian Wilderness loomed directly overhead. In addition to the Russian Wilderness, both the Marble Mountains and Trinity Alps also abut Scott Valley's flat ranchlands. It's quite a place.

Once each spring and fall, we would be awakened by a cattle drive up Main Street, which either ended or began in the Russian Mountains' high summer meadows. Within a mile of our house, Main Street deteriorated into a precarious dirt road (since paved and widened), which wound steeply upwards to a place called Etna Summit.

From Etna Summit, the gray crags of the Marbles rise to the north while the equally impressive Russian Mountains soar to the south. In between, 6000 feet below the highest peaks, the canyon of the Salmon River unfolds, the most beautiful in California. If you ever find yourself oppressed by overpopulation and urban sprawl in the Golden State, take the drive down the Salmon to Sawyers Bar and Somesbar, two of California's most remote and unspoiled towns. The drive along the Klamath River, along the Marbles' western edge from Happy Camp to Somesbar, also ranks among California's premiere scenic auto routes.

It took us less than a month, after moving to Yreka, to find our way into the Marbles. The initial foray, fittingly, landed us in the Marble Valley, which everyone assured we "just had" to see. To this day, my wife's frequent reaction, on visiting some nationally recognized scenic wonder such as Yosemite, the Trinity Alps or the Grand Canyon, is "... nice but I like the Marbles better."

Ahh, the Marbles. What can I say about them? In 1975, while waiting in the lobby of Siskiyou National Forest, in Grants Pass, Oregon, I picked up a brochure which contained a short blurb on every Wilderness Area in the National Wilderness System. It described the Marble Mountains as "a gentle wilderness, of low mountains, whose highest point is only 8300 feet."

The description was obviously written by some Washington bureaucrat who'd never been there. He (or she) failed to note that the Marbles' lowest point is 640 feet, a differential of 7540 feet. The labyrinth of ancient rock, including some of the continent's oldest, carved by glaciers into knife-edge ridges, are anything but "gentle." Trail gradients in excess of 1000 feet per mile are common. Typical is the trail to Ukonom Lake, largest lake in the Wilderness, (Chapter 9). In seven miles, it rises 800 feet, drops 1100 feet, rises 1400 feet, then drops 700 feet.

Fortunately, many routes to the Marbles' 90 lakes are a little more manageable, although others are even more difficult. Reaching Upper Wright Lake (Chapter 4), highest in the Wilderness, requires climbing 3000 feet in the first three miles. The last two miles gain yet another 1000 feet. The path to beautiful Cliff Lake (Chapter 5), second largest in the Wilderness, is much, much easier.

The Marble Mountain Wilderness ranks among California's oldest formally established Wilderness Areas. As long ago as 1931, it was set aside as a Primitive Area, being reclassified as Wilderness in 1953. Prior to the 1964 Wilderness Act, such designations were administrative only. In 1964, the original areas designated by Congress as components of the newly created National Wilderness Preservation System, proudly included the Marble Mountains of Northern California. It was enlarged in 1984.

Strangely, the Trinity Alps Primitive Area, just across the Salmon River, despite covering more than twice the area of the Marbles (525,000 acres versus 225,000 acres), with higher mountains and much more of a national reputation, was not brought into the system until 1984. While the Trinity Alps indeed rank among the most beautiful places on Earth (see "Best Hikes of the Trinity Alps," published by Mountain N'Air Books, 1992), I like the Marbles better, partly because I go back such a long way with them.

The White Russians

In between the Marbles and Trinity Alps lies the minuscule but exquisite Russian Wilderness. At 12,000 acres, it hardly compares in size to the vastness of its better known neighbors, although its highest summit, at 8196 feet, is only 100 feet lower than the Marbles' highest peak. The Russians are not a "gentle Wilderness," either.

The Russian Wilderness is centered around Russian Peak, a massive uplift of white granodiorite occupying the triangle between the North and South Forks of the Salmon River and the flat ranchlands of Scott Valley. Its dozens of lakes are far more accessible than those of the Marbles, with shorter trails and higher trailheads. The highest Russian Wilderness trailhead, to Bingham Lake (Chapter 15), lies at 7300 feet, compared to 6400 feet for the Marbles' highest trailhead (Big Meadows, Chapter 4). The Russian Wilderness's lowest elevation lies at a lofty 5080 feet.

One result of the 1984 creation of the Russian Wilderness was the naming of the range where it is located. Before that, every map had a different designation for this small but formidable cluster. Some showed it as part of the Trinity Alps, some listed it as the "Salmon-Scotts," some included it in the Scott Mountains (the ridge forming the south end of Scott Valley) and some called it the "Salmon Mountains" (even though the west end of the Trinity Alps and a major ridge in the Marbles have the same name). I am pleased to call these peaks the "Russian Mountains."

Back in 1970, the Marble and Russian Mountains were lousy with trails, even more than today. Far fewer people used them and there were fewer roads on which to reach them. Today's three mile hike often entailed seven or eight miles. Also, most trailheads weren't marked, which is definitely not the case now. You drove back and forth, or parked and beat the bushes on foot, until the trail appeared. If you couldn't find it, you tried another trail.

Current trail use in the Marbles and Russians ranges from heavy to almost nil, with some paths trod almost exclusively by cattle. Usage on the most heavily hiked paths, such as the Canyon Creek Trail to Marble Valley (Chapter 3), hardly compares to visitor numbers on trails closer to San Francisco. A peak Canyon Creek day would see less than 100 people. When I recently hiked Canyon Creek on a gorgeous Thursday in October, I had the place entirely to myself. On all but a few trails, that is likely to be the case any time of year, except during hunting season when even the most remote and mundane routes fill to overflowing.

On writing hiking guides

In my years of writing, and reading, hiking guides, I've drawn a few conclusions on how it ought to be done. First, last, sideways, upside-down, always and above all, trail descriptions should make enjoyable and interesting reading. Pointing out every rock, tree and bend in the path, in my experience, not only puts readers to sleep faster than a chloral hydrate cocktail, it is not what most readers seek. Rather than bore you with minutiae, this book attempts to capture each locale's essence, providing not only a solid reference if you do hit the dirt promenade, but readable fare if you don't. I apologize for the fact that there are only so many ways to describe a lake or an uphill climb.

Also, I warn readers that my hiking habits, like other aspects of my personality, tend to be compulsive and quirky. I collect alpine lakes the way some people collect stamps. Although hiking may be the most important thing in my life, after my wife and children, once I've reached an objective, the challenge ceases and I feel no urge to hang around, except to catch my breath before starting back.

Finally, I confess: I did not hike every single inch of the nearly 400 trail miles in the area covered by this book. That would take years and many aren't worth the trouble. I did, however, hit most of the highlights and then some. While the longest path (Wooley Creek, Chapter 8) measures 27 miles, and two or three fall in the 14 mile range, several of the best trails (Wright Lake, Marble Valley, Cliff Lake, Duck Lake), reach their destination in five miles or less. Taylor and Bingham Lakes (Chapters 11 and 14), lie only ½ mile from the trailhead.

The Marble Mountain and Russian Wilderness Areas both contain many miles of trails best described as "klunkers." A klunker is a secondary or connecting route which is extremely long, and/or does not lead to a significant destination. While many of these routes are fine if you seek solitude, a walk in the woods or a place to hunt, they don't compare to the region's best. This book has therefore exercised a certain amount of selectivity, some admittedly subjective.

Unfortunately, such selectivity can lead to problems. Since the task of preserving Wilderness is made more difficult when use is concentrated into a few highly popular areas, a Forest Service management goal is to promote disbursed use. When I recommend a popular trail and omit a seldom used one, it does not help. I strongly believe, however, that there are good reasons for the popularity of places like the Canyon Creek Trail (Chapter 3). The best I can do is alert readers to the overcrowding problem and try to include as many worthwhile off-the-beaten-path alternatives as possible.

Other than that, I've tried to present the trails in an orderly manner, breaking them into neatly tied, comprehensible bundles, without repeating myself. Bear in mind that the number of possible routes are infinite.

How to use this book

The "nuts and bolts" information on each hike is condensed at the head of each chapter. It includes:

❖ **Maps.** Readers should reach most objectives using the maps and descriptions in this book. The maps include the trail itself and the last connecting road. All are oriented with north up, unless otherwise indicated, and the scale varies with the trail length. Insets are taken from the United States Geological Survey (USGS) 7.5" (minute) topographic quadrangle maps listed in the chapter head. While USGS maps are public domain, we gladly acknowledge this invaluable source.

Supplementary material is recommended. National Forest Wilderness maps cost a couple dollars and are easily obtained. Contoured USGS and Wilderness Area maps detail steepness and minute twists and turns. The fact that I borrowed liberally from various Forest Service maps, some not generally available, in preparing this book, is gratefully acknowledged.

More and more Wilderness visitors navigate with the aid of hand-held global positioning devices, electronic instruments costing a few hundred dollars which pinpoint your location to within a few feet. These are fabulous for off-trail routes. Locations are expressed in terms of latitude and longitude. Forest Service maps show latitude and longitude in 7.5" intervals along the map edges. Each interval is the equivalent of one USGS 7.5" topo map. The 7.5" topo maps, in turn, are broken down into 2.5" minute intervals along the map edge.

To position your self on these maps, use the little crosshair X's which do not correspond to the more obvious township-range-section lines. To pinpoint map locations more precise than 2.5" (or more precise than township, range and section), it is necessary to interpolate. In my experience, it's not that difficult, even without a global positioning device. There's often a yellow metal tag nailed to a tree when a trail crosses a township, range or section line.

❖ **Destinations.**   Each chapter head lists the important destinations visited by the main trail(s) described; usually lakes, summits, meadows, cabins and rivers. They do not describe all possible destinations or trail highlights. Major destinations, the reason for taking the trail in the first place, are named in the chapter title.

❖ **Trailhead location.**   This gives the township, range and section of the trailhead, for quick map reference. A township contains 36 sections while a section consists of one square mile or 640 acres. Range designations refer to the Mount Diablo Meridian in the eastern Marbles and Russians, and the Humboldt Meridian in the western Marbles. If the range says "East," it's the Humboldt Meridian.

❖ **USGS 7.5" topo.**   This refers to the USGS map on which the trail appears, as explained under "Maps," above. Since an excellent Forest Service map is available for the Marble Mountain/Russian Wilderness Areas, USGS maps usually aren't necessary. While the USGS maps contain better topographic detail, they often aren't as up to date on trail or road locations. If you plan to take an off-trail route using a global positioning device, USGS topo maps are essential. This book contains trail corrections not shown on any current map.

❖ **E. Trail length.** Each chapter head gives length as distance from the trailhead to the farthest objective or turnaround point. Distances are rounded to the nearest ½ mile.

Since flat maps show only horizontal distance, that is the figure given. Bear in mind that a trail rising 1000 feet over a horizontal mile (5280 feet), actually spans 5373 feet. Total distance is calculated with the old high school adage, "The square of the hypotenuse (total distance) equals the sum of the squares of the other two sides (horizontal and vertical distance)." Don't forget to square root your answer.

Hiking time, being highly variable, is not given. A level mile, without pack, takes me 20 minutes while a fully loaded uphill mile can require an hour or more. While I leave many people in the dust, others leave me in the dust.

❖ **Difficulty.** An "easy" rating means the path rises at a grade of less than 5% (five feet vertical per 100 feet horizontal). "Difficult" ratings begin at 12%, or 12 vertical feet per 100 horizontal feet. Everything in-between is "moderate." Ratings may be modified by the trail's length and whether upgrades are concentrated or spread out.

A 5% grade translates to a rise of 265 feet per mile while a 12% grade gains 636 feet. The steepest trail pitches herein rise 1000 feet per mile. Short pitches, such as the top of the Marble Gap Trail (Chapter 3), approach infinity, which is one foot vertical for every zero feet horizontal, or straight up and down.

❖ **Water.** If a trail is less than two or three miles long, it's below 70 degrees out and the path is rated "easy," you probably needn't worry about water. Consider leaving a canteen or cooler in the car, however.

My rule about drinking from creeks is not to if there's habitation, cattle or horse use between me and the stream source. Since cattle grazing and horses are common in Northern California Wilderness Areas, it is best not to assume anything. Also, if I can't cross a creek in a step or two, or the water is stagnant, I won't drink from it. Icy springs in the deep woods or near a mountaintop are probably safe. However, any water can make you sick and the means through which disease is spread are myriad. So except in an emergency, it's never wise to drink unpurified water.

❖ **Season.** Since northwest California weather varies greatly, the seasons indicated are based almost entirely on elevation (modified somewhat if the entire trail climbs an exposed south or sheltered north slope), and should be considered extremely general. If it snowed down to 1000 feet a few days earlier, you should inquire before setting out on a 2000 foot elevation trail. Look for mud and high water in the wet season.

On the other hand, California winters can be marvelous, with clear, sunny days and temperatures which keep you cool yet invigorated. While most trails don't open until June or July, some lower elevation paths, such as Kelsey and Wooley Creeks (Chapters 1 and 8), remain accessible year round.

The high country offers a wonderful respite from mid-summer valley heat. Be prepared, however, for an occasional cold night. Also, summer thunderstorms, frequently born in these mountains, can be terrifying. Avoid ridgetops, open areas and standing under the highest trees if caught in a lightning storm.

❖ **Elevation.** Elevations are given in feet and most are rounded to the nearest 100. The elevations of trailheads, high and low points, significant destinations and trailheads are listed.

❖ **Use intensity.** "Light" means you're not likely to run into anybody. "Moderate" means you may encounter three or four other groups on a peak summer weekend. "Heavy" means you can expect visitors every few minutes. Bear in mind that you needn't venture far from the main paths to obtain absolute solitude and that many of the lesser used routes are as spectacular, if not more so, than the main routes. The Boulder Creek Trail to Deep Lake (Chapter 4), is a prime example.

❖ **Phone.** The number given will get you the nearest Forest Service Ranger Station rather than the Supervisor's Office. Phone ahead if you plan to bring a horse, for information on pasturing availability. Groups over 25 are not permitted.

The Marble Mountain and Russian Wilderness Areas lie entirely within Klamath National Forest. It's employees have devoted much time, money and expertise to designing, building and maintaining these routes. They are proud of their efforts and I am pleased to acknowledge them. Pertinent addresses and phone numbers are:

Supervisor's Office
1312 Fairlane Road
Eureka, CA 96097   (916) 842-6131

Salmon River Ranger District
P.O. Box 280
Etna, CA 96027   (916) 467-5757

Happy Camp Ranger District
P.O. Box 377
Happy Camp, CA 96039   (916) 493-2243

Scott River Ranger District
11263 N. Hwy 3
Fort Jones, CA 96032   (916) 468-5351

Ukonom Ranger District
P.O. Drawer 410
Orleans, CA 95556   (916) 627-3291

❖ **Directions.** This presumes you're starting from Interstate-5 in the vicinity of Yreka and follows what I believe is the shortest and/or quickest route. Before leaving home, especially if coming from Weaverville, the coast, or Oregon north of Medford, trace the route on the map to determine if it's best for you. The quickest route to Happy Camp from my home in Oregon follows a maze of secondary roads completely bypassing I-5 and Highway-96, the route given in the book.

About hiking

Before getting to the standard list of hiking do's and don'ts required in all books of this nature, let me offer a few unscientific observations on a variety of subjects:

- Since hiking provides a means of getting in shape, lack of previous conditioning shouldn't dissuade you. Start on "easy" or "moderate" paths and take your time. If you have a heart condition or other limitation, consult your physician first.

In my experience, weight control (and avoiding cigarettes) contributes more to negotiating a steep trail than does leg conditioning. I say this having hiked in all possible combinations of obesity, slimness, in shape-ness and out of shape-ness. A consistent upper body program, combined with diet and a little jogging or pace walking, should keep the average person in shape for most trails herein. You'd be amazed at the effect of upper body strength on lung capacity.

Physical stress is not confined to uphill tracks. The overweight or out of shape person is likely to notice upgrades more because they stress the cardiovascular system. Steep downgrades stress the knees, ankles and feet. That's when most blisters occur, which can ruin a trip far more quickly than huffing and puffing. With a touch of arthritis in one hip, downgrades bother me more than upgrades.

- As I settle into middle age, I've developed a paranoia about dehydration. Back in my 20's, when nothing tired me out, it didn't bother me when my mouth got a little dry. These days, I worry about blood pressure, respiration and pulse rates, the color of my urine (dark yellow indicates dehydration), electrolytes, etc. I sip water constantly as I hike and have been known to slip a little Gatorade in my canteen.

Foods with high water content are best and small, nibbly snacks get it into your blood stream fastest. Since foods cut into bite sized portions get chewed more thoroughly, bring apple slices rather than a whole apple. Peanut butter and jelly sandwiches, cookies, cheese sticks and the redoubtable trail mix are all dandy, provided you keep the portions down. Liquefied foods are marvelous. Try topping your meals with orange or V8 juice.

- The once popular heavy hiking boots with non-skid, Vibram soles are somewhat out of vogue. They can be environmentally damaging and should be worn only when rock climbing, in snow, or off the trail in wet weather. I find a soft-soled sneaker much more comfortable and less tiring, although I jab an ankle in them occasionally.

- I've always carried a few Band-Aids on my treks but have yet to use them, except to cover the spot on my right foot, between my middle and third toes, which always seems to blister. I prefer band-aids to moleskin for blisters because moleskin is designed for use before the blister develops and can be painful to remove afterwards.

- While high quality camping gear can greatly add to the comfort of your trip, the lack thereof need not preclude venturing into the wilderness. I carry minimal gear when I hike, most of it well worn. I nearly always eat cold meals and I never build a campfire. Good and sufficient equipment, however, is essential if there's the slightest chance of rain, snow, the temperature dropping below freezing or if you plan to be gone more than a day or two.

While most summer trips are uneventful, one hike for this book reminded me how precarious wilderness can be. I made the seven mile trek to Ukonom Lake (Chapter 9), on a sunny, late August day where the temperature in Yreka had reached 84. Since my daughter took my good sleeping bag to college with her (without asking), I used an old lightweight one we had around the house. The closest thing to a jacket I brought was a flannel shirt. Two weeks prior, both the shirt and the lightweight sleeping bag served me just fine at Sky High Lake.

That night, unexpectedly, the temperature at Ukonom Lake dropped below freezing. Every time I ventured out of my sleeping bag, I ended up shivering uncontrollably. Even after scurrying back in, it took several minutes to stop shaking and get my nose and fingers warm. From 3:00 AM on, I couldn't get my feet warm no matter what.

When I headed out in the morning, my feet were numb for the first ½ mile. Although there was no damage, it was more than a little frightening. The advice later given me was to pack up and leave as soon as the problem with my feet started. Either that or build a fire. An electric foot warmer or really good wool socks, would have done wonders. Brrrr.

- No hiking book is complete without a rules list: Never hike alone. Always bring matches. Inform someone of your destination. Never drink unpurified water. Get a doctor's OK. Carry toilet paper. Never leave home without map, canteen, whistle (which I could never figure out), compass (which I've never needed...so far), rope for hanging bear bags, etc.

  I rarely observe the above, except for carrying water. Usually, I hike alone and neglect to tell my wife my destination. Half the time I forget map, camera, canteen, lunch and gas money. I've gotten sick, lost, injured and stuck on my excursions but somehow always make it back. To me, it's part of the adventure. But as the frozen feet episode demonstrated, I could be courting disaster.

- A friend thinks I'm nuts for not carrying a pistol when I hike; for use against bears, rattlesnakes and psychopaths. In the first place, I wouldn't know how to use one. In the second place, they're way too heavy. And in the third place, they wouldn't stop a bear and I couldn't bring myself to shoot a rattlesnake.

  I admit, though, that on one or two occasions, I've run into human situations where a weapon would have been comforting. In every instance, I didn't need it and was probably far better off without it. Almost to a person, hikers are a friendly, helpful bunch who love to chat and share information.

- Over the years, I've received phone calls and letters, some miffed, from readers unable to find trailheads, or who got lost on the trail, or who expressed some complaint or other. Fortunately, most people who spot the rare errors in my books are simply interested in passing the information along.

  While I love hearing from readers, and while I do my best to keep my information up to date, accurate and clear, I believe that they, not me, are responsible for the outcome of their journeys. Remember that part of the charm and adventure of these mountains is that things change. Roads may be gated without notice or become washed out or blocked, forests burn, boundaries get moved, things dry up or get muddy, bridges deteriorate or disappear, trails become overgrown, trailhead and road markers vanish, new roads and trails get built.

These uncertainties, to me, enhance the experience. If I'm unable to reach an objective, which happens from time to time, I simply go somewhere else or go home.

- Finally, the Forest Service offers a list of camping guidelines far more important than mine. As part of "no trace" camping, they ask the following:

1. Pack out all litter.

2. For human waste, select a spot at least 200 feet from open water and dig a hole six to eight inches deep. Cover it with dirt when done. (Personally, I'm not about to carry a shovel, although a garden trowel would suffice. If you must know, I find an extremely secluded place, well away from trails and streams. When done, I kick dirt over it and drop the largest rock I can find on top of it.)

3. If a fire is absolutely necessary, build it in a safe, previously used spot, preferably a fire ring at an established campsite. Wood collection can be environmentally damaging and portable stoves are recommended. Cold meals are best.

4. Pitch tents so no drainage ditch is required and replace rocks and other material removed from sleeping areas. Camp sites should be at least 100 feet from open water and animals should be pastured at least 200 feet from open water.

About the land

The descriptions herein include a trove of natural history. Since several trails may penetrate the same area, and since each description is written to stand on its own, some repetition was unavoidable. While natural history is often described in detail, listing the identifying traits of every rock type, tree species and flower at each mention, would take far too much space.

The following concepts, for the most part, failed to find their way into the chapters or are spread thinly among many.

- ❖ **Geology.** Three major geological provinces are represented in Northwest California: The Cascade Mountains, the Klamath Mountains and the Mendocino (or Coast Range) Mountains. Of these, the most spectacular and best known are the Cascades, a north-south trending string of volcanoes capped by 14,161 foot Mount Shasta, Northern California's highest peak.

The Klamath Mountains, of which the Marbles and Russians are components, rank as northern California's oldest and most rugged. Dating from the Mesozoic Era (200 million years ago), they consist of an immense granitic intrusion (granite is molten rock which hardened before working its way to the surface), possibly formed as part of the Sierra Nevada range. The Klamath Mountains' most common granitic rock is granodiorite. Other Klamath rocks include an ancient, partially metamorphosed (structurally altered over a long time period) lava known as greenstone or metavolcanic rock, plus scattered outcroppings of schist and marble, which are also metamorphosed rocks but with different parent materials.

Marble is metamorphosed limestone. Limestone, in turn, is an ocean sediment composed of seashells and other organisms made of calcium carbonate. As a sedimentary rock, it tends to ride on top of the granites and schists, which work their way up from underneath. Both marble and limestone are prone to dissolving out and forming caves. Marble caves contain more vertical shafts than limestone caves but limestone caves are usually larger.

A rock known as serpentinite also abounds in the Marbles. Serpentinite is a granitic rock lacking calcium and rich in heavy metals. The Klamath and Mendocino Mountains contain more of this rock than any other region of the United States (although the largest serpentinite formation occurs in Alaska's Brooks Range). Serpentinite is the basement rock of the ocean floor. On land, it appears as elongated dikes and sills parallel to the coast. Such formations are believed to have been bulldozed from the sea by the advancing continental plate. The greenish-black rock weathers to a buff orange color.

Douglas-fir, ponderosa pine, madrone and other common species won't grow on serpentinite or are stunted by it. Other species love it, however, including Jeffrey pine, knobcone pine, white pine, incense cedar and Baker cypress. In the Klamath

Mountains, Jeffrey pine occurs only on serpentinite. Numerous endangered shrubs and wildflowers grow nowhere else.

Several theories explain how the Klamath Mountains came into being. The "Klamath Island" theory postulates that the ancient range broke loose from the Sierra a zillion years ago and drifted out to sea, spending eons as a 20,000 square mile offshore island. Other theories suggest a subterranean connection between the Sierra, the Klamaths and Oregon's Blue and Wallowa Mountains. Or these ranges may be totally unrelated. The Klamath system's highest peak is Mount Eddy, rising to 9045 not far from Mount Shasta.

Most northwest California peaks over 5000 feet have experienced glaciation. Glaciers form when snowfall exceeds melt and ice starts oozing down the mountain. The only glaciers these days are on Shasta, plus a few tiny ones in the Trinity Alps. Gouged out scars from former glaciers abound, however.

Glaciers not only carve out round-bottomed valleys as they move downward, they chisel sharply backward into the peak. This headword cutting creates "cirque" basins with steep, amphitheater headwalls rising above a bowl. Almost all alpine lakes in the Marble and Russian Mountains, occupy glacial cirques.

❖ **Botany.** More important than memorizing long species lists, in understanding the botany of Northern California, is the concept of "associations." This refers to different plant species which predictably grow alongside one another in similar kinds of places. For example, while you'll never find black oak and mountain hemlock in the same stand; Douglas-fir and black oak hang out together all the time.

Associations range from the broadly geographic to the highly site specific. Several major geographic associations, or bio-regions, cross northwest California: The Pacific Northwest forest region (Douglas-fir, mountain hemlock, whitebark pine, Western white pine, Oregon white oak, Pacific madrone), the Sierra Nevada forest region (Douglas-fir, sugar pine, incense cedar, white fir, foxtail pine), the Northern Coastal forest region (Pacific yew, tanoak, canyon live oak), and the California Coastal forest region (California black oak, bay laurel).

Look also for riverbank associations, serpentine associations, upland associations, bog associations, north slope associations (shady), south slope associations (sunny), elevational associations, etc.

The trail descriptions spend the most time on elevational associations. It's fascinating to observe the transition as a trail begins down in the oaks, madrones and Douglas-firs; works its way through the red firs, white pines and mountain hemlocks; and ends up in the foxtail pines and whitebark pines adorning the highest ridgetops.

The Klamath Mountains region, and the Russian Mountains in particular, are well known to botanists for their extreme diversity. Some 25 conifer species and over 1500 herbaceous species have been listed for Siskiyou County, California, where the Marbles and Russians are located. Three factors combine to create this: (1) The Klamath Mountains, as noted, lie in an overlap between several major geographic bio-regions. (2) The region contains large areas of serpentinite rock, on which many common species will not grow. (3) Extreme glaciation during the last Ice Age played havoc with the natural ranges of numerous species.

Of interest are the presence of "glacial relics," isolated populations of species whose main range lies hundreds of miles north or south. Virtually the only California occurrences of Engelmann spruce, Pacific silver fir and subalpine fir lie in the Russian Mountains. Similarly, foxtail pine's main stomping grounds is the eastern High Sierra. After a 600 mile gap, it turns up sporadically in the Marbles, Russians and Trinity Alps.

The Klamath Mountains boast several unique species, including Brewer spruce, Sadler oak, wing-seeded draba, Salmon Mountains wake-robin, Marble Mountain catchfly and many others. Knobcone pine, Shasta red fir and tanoak don't extend far outside the region. Since the Marbles and Russians have been only lightly explored by botanists, new species and subspecies are discovered fairly regularly.

Northern California's rarest tree is Baker cypress. The Marbles' two minuscule Baker cypress stands both lie outside the Wilderness boundary, well away from any road or trail. One is on the ridge above Kuntz Creek, near the Klamath River town of Hamburg, the other lies on the ridge above Little Elk Creek (Chapter 10). More extensive stands occur on the serpentinite slopes directly across the Klamath, up Seiad Creek.

Like Baker cypress, digger pine is found in the Marbles but not inside the Wilderness. Look for this scraggly foothill species, briefly, along the Salmon River Road near Forks of Salmon. It is identified by immense, pineapple shaped cones.

Finally, there is a raging controversy regarding California red fir *(Abies magnifica)*, Shasta red fir *(Abies magnifica var. shastensis)* and noble fir *(Abies procera)*, which are extremely similar and hybridize with each other. While 80% to 90% of red firs in the Marbles and Russians are California reds, nearly all have some Shasta red or noble traits. Those at the highest elevations, especially to the north, show the most noble fir traits. When I use the term "red fir," it refers to all three species.

While my main expertise as a naturalist is trees and shrubs, that is not why I devote more space to them than to herbaceous plants. It's just that there are so many herbaceous species, they're difficult to list without lapsing into a boring recitation. Also, when you hike a trail in August and September or later, most wildflowers are no longer in bloom.

I would love to have included a complete, illustrated botanical key to the 1750 species of conifers, hardwoods, wildflowers, grasses and other plants found in Siskiyou County. The following list, lengthy as it is, doesn't come close to being comprehensive since we're talking about one of North America's most botanically diverse areas. In any given square mile, you're likely to turn up 500 species. For those unfamiliar with the local botanical denizens, try looking up some of the following before taking to the trail:

CONIFERS
Cypress Family
Incense cedar *(Calocedrus decurrens)*
Port Orford cedar *(Chamaecyparis lawsoniana)*
Baker cypress *(Cupresssus bakerii)*
Common juniper *(Juniperis communis)*
Western juniper *(Juniperis occidentalis)*
Pine Family
Digger pine *(Pinus sabiniana)*
Foxtail pine *(Pinus balfouriana)*
Jeffrey pine *(Pinus jeffreyii)*
Knobcone pine *(Pinus attenuata)*
Lodgepole pine *(Pinus contorta)*
Ponderosa pine *(Pinus ponderosa)*
Sugar pine *(Pinus lambertiana)*
Western white pine *(Pinus monticola)*
Whitebark pine *(Pinus albicaulis)*
Noble fir *(Abies procera)*
California red fir *(Abies magnifica)*
Shasta red fir *(Abies magnifica v shastensis)*
Pacific silver fir *(Abies amabilis)*
Subalpine fir *(Abies lasiocarpa)*
White fir *(Abies concolor)*
Brewer spruce *(Picea breweriana)*
Engelmann spruce *(Picea engelmannii)*
Douglas-fir *(Pseudotsuga menziesii)*
Mountain hemlock *(Tsuga mertensiana)*
Yew Family
Pacific yew *(Taxus brevifolia)*

HARDWOODS
Barberry Family
Dwarf oregongrape *(Berberis nervosa)*
Creeping oregongrape *(Berberis repens)*
Beech Family
Golden chinkapin *(Castanopsis chrysophylla)*
Tanoak *(Lithocarpus densifloris)*
California black oak *(Quercus kelloggii)*
Canyon liveoak *(Quercus chrysolepis)*
Interior liveoak *(Quercus wislizeni)*
Oregon white oak *(Quercus garryana)*
Sadler oak *(Quercus sadlerii)*

Birch Family
> Mountain alder *(Alnus tenuifolia)*
> Red alder *(Alnus rubra)*
> White alder *(Alnus rhombifolia)*
> Hazelnut *(Coryulus cornuta)*

Buckthorn Family
> Deerbrush/buckbrush *(Ceanothus integerrimus,*
> > C. thrysifloris, C. sanguineus)
> Snowbrush (Ceanothus velutinus)
> Squawcarpet (Ceanothus prostratus)
> Whitethorn (Ceanothus cuneatus)
> California coffeeberry (Rhamnus californica)

Cashew Family
> Poison oak (Toxicodendron diversiloba)

Currant Family
> Red flowering currant (Ribes sanguineum)
> Prickly gooseberry (Ribes lacustre)

Dogwood Family
> Pacific dogwood (Cornus nuttallii)
> Western dogwood (Cornus stolonifera)

Heath Family
> Western azalea (Rhododendron occidentale)
> Red mountain heather (Phyllodoce impetriformis)
> White heather (Cassiope mertensiana)
> Evergreen huckleberry (Vaccinium ovatum)
> Red huckleberry (Vaccinium parvifolium)
> Whortleberry (Vaccinium membranaceum)
> Labrador tea (Ledum glandulosum)
> Pacific madrone (Arbutus menziesii)
> Green manzanita (Arctostaphylos patula)
> Pinemat manzanita (Arctostaphylos nevadensis)
> White manzanita (Arctostaphylos viscida)
> Pacific rhododendron (Rhododendron macrophyllum)
> Salal (Gaultheria sp.)

Honeysuckle Family
> Blue elderberry (Sambucus cerulea)
> Honeysuckle (Lonicera involucrata)
> Snowberry (Symphoricarpos albus)

Laurel Family
> California laurel (Umbellularia californica)

Maple Family
> Bigleaf maple (Acer macrophyllum)

Rocky Mountain maple (Acer glabrum)
Vine maple (Acer circinatum)
Olive family
Oregon ash (Fraxinus latifolia)
Rose Family
Cutleaf blackberry (Rubus laciniatus)
Himalayaberry (Rubus discolor)
Wild blackberry (Rubus ursinus)
Blackcap raspberry (Rubus leucodermis)
Thimbleberry (Rubus parvifloris)
Western mountain-ash (Sorbus scopulina)
Bittercherry (Prunus emarginata)
Chokecherry (Prunus virginiana)
Curl-leaf mountain-mahogany (Cercocarpus ledifolius)
Oceanspray (Holodiscus discolor)
Little wood rose (Rosa gymnocarpa)
Pacific serviceberry (Amelanchier alnifolia)
Douglas spirea (Spirea douglasii)
Wild strawberry (Fragaria californica)
Silktassel Family
Silktassel (Garrya sp.)
Staff-Tree Faimly
Oregon boxwood (Pachystima myrsinites)
Sunflower Family
Rabbitbrush (Chrysothamnus sp.)
Sagebrush (Artemesia sp.)
Willow Family
Quaking aspen (Populus tremuloides)
Black cottonwood (Populus trichocarpa)
Willow (Salix sp.)

HERBACEOUS PLANTS
Amaryllis Family
Wild onion (Allium sp.)
Brodeia (Brodeia sp.)
Barberry Family
Vanillaleaf (Achlys triphylla)
Bedstraw Family
Bedstraw (Galium bifolium)
Bleeding Heart Family
Bleeding heart (Dicentra formosa)

Bluebell Family
> California bluebell (Campanula prenanthoides)

Broomrape Family
> Dwarfmistletoe (Arceuthobium douglasii)
> Ground cone flower (Boschniakia strobilacea)
> Broomrape (Orobanche uniflora)

Buckwheat Family
> Eriogonum (Eriogonum sp.)
> Naked stem buckwheat (Polygonum sp.)
> Sheep sorrel (Rumex acetosella)

Bur-reed Family
> Bur-reed (Sparganium angustiolium)

Buttercup Family
> W. Baneberry (Actaea rubra)
> Buttercup (Ranunculus sp.)
> Columbine (Aquilegia formosa)
> Delphinium (Delphinium sp.)
> Marsh marigold (Caltha leptosepala)
> Monkshood (Aconitum columbianum)
> W. Pasqueflower (Anemone occidentalis)
> Columbia windflower (Anemone deltoidea)

Carrot Family
> Angelica (Angelica tomentosa)
> Cow parsnip (Heracleum sphondylium)
> Lomatium (Lomatium sp.)
> Sierra snakeroot (Sanicula graveolens)
> Sweet cicely (Osmorrhiza occidentalis)
> Yampah (Periderida gairdneri)

Dogbane Family
> Dogbane (Apocynum pumila)

Evening Primrose Family
> Clarkia (Clarkia rhomboidea)
> Red fireweed (Epilobium angustifolium)

Forget-Me-Not Family
> Hound's tongue (Cynoglossum occidentale)
> Stickseed (Hackelia micrantha)
> Lungwort (Mertensia oblongifolia)

Gentian Family
> Explorer's gentian (Gentiana calycosa)
> Mendocino gentian (Gentiana setigera)
> Newberry's gentian (Gentiana newberrii)
> Monument plant (Frasera speciosa)

Geranium Family
Richardson's geranium (Geranium richardsonii)
Sticky geranium (Geranium viscosissum)
Honeysuckle Family
Snowberry (Symphorcarpos sp.)
Twinflower (Linnaea borealis)
Iris Family
Wild iris (Iris sp.)
Lily Family
Bear grass (Xerophyllum tenax)
Cat's ear (Calochortus sp.)
Fairy bell (Disporum hookeri)
Fritillary (Fritillaria sp.)
Corn lily (Veratrum californicum)
Fawn lily (Erythronium grandiflorum)
Tiger lily (Lilium sp.)
Washington lily (Lilium washingtonianum)
Queen's cup (Clintonia uniflora)
Soap plant (Chlorogalum sp.)
Solomon's seal (Smilacina sp.)
W. stenanthum (Stenanthum occidentalis)
Trillium (Trillium sp.)
Twisted stick (Streptopus amplexifolius)
Mallow Family
Oregon sidelcea (Sidelcea oregana)
Mint Family
Rigid hedge nettle (Stachys rigida)
Nettleleaf horsemint (Agastache urticifolia)
Mint (Mondarella sp.)
Pennyroyal (Mentha pulegium)
Self-heal (Prunella vulgaris)
Skullcap (Scutellaria californica)
W. verbena (Verbena lasiostachys)
Mustard Family
W. Bittercress (Cardamine oligosperma)
Yellow cress (Rorippa obtusa)
Draba (Draba sp.)
Milkmaid (Dentaria californica)
Mountain jewel (Streptanthus tortuosus)
W. tansy mustard (Descuriania richardsonii)
Rockcress (Arabis sp.)
W. wallflower (Erysimum occidentale)

Orchid Family
>Mertans coralroot (Corallorhiza bulbosa)
>Spotted coralroot (Corallorhiza maculata)
>Hooded lady's tresses (Spiranthes porrifolia)
>Calypso orchid (Calypso bulbosa)
>Rattlesnake orchid (Goodyera oblongifolia)
>Rein orchid (Habernia sp.)
>Calif. lady's slipper (Cypripedium californicum)
>Broad-lipped twinblade (Listera convallaroides)

Pea Family
>Clover (Trifolium sp.)
>Lotus (Lotus sp.)
>Lupine (Lupinus sp.)
>Pursh's sheepspod (Astragalus purshii)
>American vetch (Vicia americana)

Phlox Family
>Grand collomia (Collomia grandiflora)
>Vari-leaf collomia (Collomia heterophylla)
>Blue-headed gilia (Gilia capitata)
>Slender phlox (Microsteris gracilis)
>Spreading phlox (Phlox diffusa)
>Showy polemium (Polemium pulcherrimum)

Pink Family
>Indian pink (Silene californica)
>Gray's catchfly (Silene grayi)
>Meadow chickweed (Cerastium arvense)
>Ballhead sandwort (Arnaria congesta)

Pitcher Plant Family
>Darlingtonia (Darlingtonia californica)

Primrose Family
>Shooting star (Dodecatheon jeffreyi)

Purslane Family
>Lewisia (Lewisia sp.)
>Littleleaf montia (Montia parvifolia)
>Siberian candyflower (Montia sibirica)
>Miner's lettuce (Montia perfoliata)
>Pussy paw (Calyptridium umbellatum)

Rose Family
>Cinquefoil (Potentilla sp.)
>Partridge foot (Luetkea pectinata)
>Prairie smoke (Geum cioliatum)
>Gordon's Ivesia (Ivesia gordonii)

Saxifrage Family
    Boykinea (Boykinea major)
    Fringe cup (Tellima grandiflora)
    Grass of parnassus (Parnassia sp.)
    Saxifrage (Saxifraga sp.)
    Umbrella plant (Peltiphyllum peltatum)
Sedum Family
    Sierra sedum (Sedium obtusatum)
Snapdragon Family
    Giant blue-eyed mary (Collinsia parviflora)
    Alpine brooklime (Veronica alpine)
    American brooklime (Veronica americana)
    Coiled lousewort (Pedicularis contorta)
    Parrot's beak (Pedicularis recemosa)
    Copeland's owl clover (Orthocarpus copelandii)
    Indian paintbrush (Castilleja sp.)
    Seep-spring monkey flower (Mimulus gattatus)
    Lewis's monkey flower (Mimulus lewisii)
    Mtn. monkey flower (Mimulus tilingii)
    Pentstemon (Pentstemon sp.)
Sunflower Family
    Arnica (Arnica sp.)
    Cascade aster (Aster ledophyllus)
    Balsamroot (Balsamorhiza hookeri)
    Butterweed (Senecio sp.)
    Daisy (Erigeron sp.)
    Everlasting (Antennaria sp.)
    Hawksbeard (Crepis acuminata)
    Meadow goldenrod (Solidago canadensis)
    Madia (Madia sp.)
    Microseris (Microseris nutans)
    Mule ears (Wyethia mollis)
    Ox-eye daisy (Chrysanthemum leucanthemum)
    Bigelow's sneezeweed (Helium bigelovii)
    Sunflower (Helianthum gracilentus)
    Wooly sunflower (Eriophyllum lanatum)
    Bull thistle (Cirisium vulgare)
    Yarrow (Achilla lanulosa)
Valerian Family
    Mountain valerian (Valeriana sitchensis)
Violet Family
    Violet (Viola sp.)

Waterleaf Family
   Silverleaf phacelia (Phacelia hastata)
   California waterleaf (Hydrophyllum occidentalis)
Water Lily Family
   Pond lily (Nuphar polysepalum)
Wintergreen Family
   Pine drop (Pterospora andromeda)
   Little prince's pine (Chimaphila menziesii)
   W. prince's pine (Chimaphila umbellata)
   Sugarstick (Allotropa virgata)
   Snowplant (Sarcodes secunda)
   Wintergreen (Pyrola sp.)

Mammals

Observation of wildlife is a prime reason people take to the Wilderness. While most mammals, except for deer and chipmunks, tend to be elusive, a sharp eye frequently pays off. Following are random comments on Northern California's most common mammals. It presumes you know what the species looks like.

Opossum. This sluggish marsupial, which has a terrible problem steering clear of cars, does well in a surprising variety of environments. It nests in hollow trees and rock crevices and can use its tail for swinging. The species was introduced to Western North America at the turn of the century. Don't ask me why.

Deer. The Columbian blacktail, second smallest deer variety in North America, belongs to the same family as domestic cattle. Since it has a cloven hoof and chews its cud, it is the Marbles' only kosher wildlife species (there are no mountain goats or bighorn sheep).

This highly adaptable species turns up in many low and middle elevation environments, especially open areas with forest cover nearby, which means they benefit from logging clearcuts. In the Marbles, deer can get extremely pesky, prowling the edge of campsites in quest of salt and food. Fortunately, most campers are more intrigued than annoyed by their presence. Do not feed them.

Elk. Yes, there are elk in the areas covered by this book, but they're extremely scarce. These majestic creatures are California's largest land mammal. In contrast to the diminutive blacktail, a bull elk can stand seven feet tall at the shoulder, with antlers five feet long. They have a much stronger herding tendency than deer.

Cattle.   These are the bane of the Marbles, turning up in nearly every basin with open meadows. Aside from destroying the ecosystem and poisoning the water, they're harmless.

Although I can't imagine why a 1000 pound cow would fear a human, they invariably run off when a hiker approaches. Sharing a campsite with a herd of cattle can be annoying. They moo loudly and often at dusk and in the morning, although a loud yell usually gets rid of them.

Bear.   The story of how the last grizzly was run out of California is well known. Suffice to say, any bear you run across will be a black bear, a much less aggressive species. I've seen two bears on the trail (plus two from the car), in my years of wilderness hiking, although I worry about them a lot. Bear sign turns up often, usually in the form of seed laden droppings.

While I've never had a bear enter my camp, or heard of anybody being injured by one without extreme provocation (they usually hightail it if they see a human), they are not to be trifled with. They frequently rummage through camps in quest of food and have been known to damage parked cars if they see something edible through the window. The Forest Service recommends that you hang all food at night, well away from your campsite and well out of reach.

Cougar.   These may be the most beautiful, and elusive, of California's large mammals. I've been pretty lucky, having seen cougar five times over the years. Many veteran hikers have never been so honored. The cougar is North America's largest cat. Despite its secretive behavior, it is found in virtually every state.

Bobcat.   Bobcats are much smaller than cougars and you're far more likely to encounter one. They have stubby tails and pointed ears.

Coyote.   These relatives of the wolf and dog are extremely common in Northern California, although they prefer open range and desert to high mountains. They're much more solitary than wolves and eat mostly small rodents.

Fox. I've seen only one fox in the wild but it was well worth the wait. Its huge, fluffy tail would put the average squirrel to shame. This canine species is more cat-like than dog-like in its behavior. Although lacking retractable claws, it stalks, pounces and climbs trees.

Raccoon. This common, adorable animal can be a pest, raiding camps and chewing through and rifling packs. It's another good reason to hang your food at night. Unless you sneak up on one of these nocturnal critters with a flashlight, you're not likely to meet once face to face. Raccoons belong to the same mammalian order as dogs (Carnivora), and are compatible with human populations.

Rats and mice. These are by far the most abundant mammals. They hold the unenviable distinction of occupying the bottom of the food chain (although their populations are so enormous, the likelihood of a given mouse getting eaten is slim).

Despite their numbers, you're unlikely to run across one since they're nocturnal and extremely wary. Don't look for the familiar European house mouse or Norway rat in the wilderness. More likely, you'll find an All-American variety with a furry tail, such as a kangaroo rat, harvest mouse or meadow vole.

Wood rat. You're more apt to encounter the nest of one of these fat, fascinating creatures than the actual animal. Look for a haphazard pile of sticks, usually in the deep woods, up to three feet high. Also referred to as "pack rats," they have an affinity for shiny objects.

Squirrel/ground squirrel/chipmunk. Being day feeders, 90% of mammals seen from the trail will fall into one of these categories of nut munchers. Tree squirrels are the guys with big bushy tails (except for flying squirrels), who climb trees. Ground squirrels can have small bushy tails or no bushy tails and come in either plain or striped wrappers. Some can also climb trees. All chipmunks are striped. Unlike striped ground squirrels, the stripe extends to the head.

Beaver. As with woodrats, you're more likely to notice the works of beavers than the animal itself. Beaver dams, impoundments and lodges are a unique treat even if their creators never poke their noses out of the water.

Muskrat. This aquatic mammal hangs out in still waters along riverbanks. It is trapped for its fur and secretes a musk scent used in perfumes.

Porcupine. Porkies became my favorite mammal following a zoo demonstration. The slow, wary beasts can reach up to 40 pounds. Despite their infamous defense mechanism, they can be quite friendly under the right circumstances. They adore dining on young growth forests, much to the chagrin of foresters.

Rabbits. Bunnies are smaller than hares and behave differently. The former nest in underground dens while the latter nest above ground in shallow depressions. You're more likely to see a cottontail while hiking, since hares prefer open county.

Bigfoot. I love the idea of bigfoot and am convinced that a large, intelligent, herbivorian primate could exist undetected in the back country of the Northwest. Especially when you consider that the 400 miles of trail in the Marbles barely scratch the surface. I've never seen a bigfoot but know people who have. Don't try to tell them it was their imagination or a bear.

Rattlesnakes. While the average reader can live without detailed information on the rough skinned newt or blue tailed skink, the Western rattlesnake is another matter. Only our friend the brown bear evokes more curiosity, rumor and apprehension.

There's little to worry about. In my half-dozen rattlesnake encounters, they've been more anxious than I to avoid confrontation. Do keep an eye out for them in grass, brush or when stepping over logs or rocks. Should you spot (or hear) one, walk a wide berth around it. They're pretty slow and have a striking range of only a couple feet.

If you get chomped, the recommended treatment is to apply ice and get to a doctor within two hours. Keep in mind that (a), they don't always get the venom out and (b), a healthy adult can usually shake off a snake bite. Victims should avoid walking for several hours. If a small child or someone with asthma or a heart condition gets bitten, it should be taken extremely seriously.

The practice of killing rattlesnakes for no reason is, to me, unconscionable. Bear in mind that you're the intruder, not the snake.

Lake summary/angling information

Since I couldn't catch a fish to save my life, any assessment I might make on fishing would be useless. I hasten to add that for most anglers, the high lakes of the Marbles and Russians, and wilderness streams such as Wooley Creek and the North Fork of the Salmon, offer some of the premiere fishing experiences anywhere.

The vast majority of California's alpine lakes contain Eastern brook and/or rainbow trout. A few yield an occasional brown or golden trout. In the major streams and rivers, look for trout higher up, with steelhead, king and silver salmon, a few minnows and the inevitable suckers and eels lower down. Bass and sunfish sometimes turn up in low elevation, warm waters.

Most high (and low) lakes in Northern California are stocked annually, or nearly annually, by the California Department of Fish and Game. You'd be amazed at the remote pools they visit on their aerial drops of finny fingerlings. Few high lakes boast honest to gosh native fish populations since there's no way a trout could find its way to a place like Bingham Lake without ropes and carabiniers. Furthermore, there is little natural reproduction in most lakes, either by planted or native stock.

You can tell from their names that Eastern brook and German brown trout are not West Coast natives. Only the common rainbow trout calls the region's high creeks and lakes home, but only lakes with a navigable outlet and streams free of barriers.

In preparing this book, I relied heavily on a pair of pamphlets called "Angler's Guide to the Marble Mountains," and "Angler's Guide to the Salmon and Scott Mountains," put out by the California Department of Fish and Game. They haven't been available in years. I stashed away a few copies when I worked for the Department in 1970.

The best fishing lakes contain greenish water and much shoreline and aquatic vegetation, but not so much that the lake is unfishable or inaccessible. Ideally, they will contain shallow areas along the edge, a few logs, a fair amount of cover and a deep spot.

The following list is confined to lakes mentioned in the text, which contain fish. It includes 95% of the lakes in the Marbles and Russians.

LAKE	Chapt	Acres	Depth	Elev.	COMMENTS
Abbott Lk.	7	8	20	5650	Rocky shore, brook trout
Lower Albers Lk.	12	2.5	15	6900	Brook trout
U. Albers Lk.	12	2	15	7150	Brook and rainbow
Aspen Lk	4	5.5	58	7100	Rock ledge shore, brook trout
Bear Lk.	2	2	8	5950	Brushy shore, brook trout
Big Blue Lk.	11	17	96	6800	Steep, very rocky shore, rainbow and brown
Bingham Lk.	14	8.5	55	7050	Steep shore, brook and rainbow and brow
Blueberry Lk.	6	1.5	10	6050	Brushy, open shore; brook trout.
Buckhorn Lk.	4	2	25	7100	Rock ledge shore, brook and rainbow
Burney Lk.	3	15	25	5650	Wooded shore, brook trout, natural repro
Calf Lk.	5	3	30	7000	Rocky, open shore; brook trout
Campbell Lk.	5	33	30	5800	Wooded shore; brook, rainbow and brown
Chimney Rock	7	5.5	22	6100	Steep, mostly wooded shore; brook and rainbow
Chinquapi	4	3.5	25	7150	Open, very rocky shore; brook and rainbow
Clear Lk.	7	6.5	62	5400	Level, brushy shore, very clear water; large brook, rainbow, brown
Cliff Lk.	5	52	175	6100	Open shore; brook, rainbow and brown
Cuddihy Lk.	9	3.5	18	5650	Grassy shore, brook trout
Cuddihy Lk. #2	9	1	5	5650	Level, grassy shore; brook trout
Cuddihy Lk. #3	9	7	20	5700	Grassy, somewhat wooded shore; brook trout
Cuddihy Lk. #4	9	2.5	20	5700	Brushy, rocky shore; brook and rainbow
Deadman Lk.	9	9	25	5700	Rocky, brushy shore with open woods; brook trout
Deep Lk.	4	16	68	6350	Open, grassy shore; brook, rainbow and brown
Big Duck Lk.	13	26	27	6400	Wooded, rocky shore; brook and rainbow
Little Duck Lk.	13	5	18	6700	Wooded shore, brook trout
Eaton Lk.	13	13	27	6600	Level, wooded shore; rainbow trout
Big Elk Lk.	3	4.5	10	6050	Meadowy shore; rainbow and brown
Little Elk Lk.	3	6	5	5400	Open shore, rainbow and brown, natural repr

LAKE	Chapt	Acres	Depth	Elev.	COMMENTS
English Lk.	7	6.5	28	5750	Wooded shore, brook trout
Ethel Lk.	7	9	22	5700	Brushy shore, brook trout
Fisher Lk.	6	1	15	6200	Meadowed shore, brook and rainbow
Blue Granite Lk.	9	12	28	5250	Brushy, wooded shore; brook and rainbow. Brook trout in outlet creek
Gold Granite Lk.	9	2	14	5600	Level, brushy shore; brook and rainbow
Green Granite Lk.	9	4	11	5600	Brushy shore, brook and rainbow
Hancock Lk.	7	44	56	6350	Open, rock ledge shore; brook trout
High Lk.	14	4.5	55	7300	Wooded shore, brook and rainbow
Hogan Lk.	11	7.5	26	5950	Wooded and grassy shore, brook and rainbow, natural repro
Hooligan Lk.	9	95	17	5150	Very brushy shore, brook trout
Horse Range Lk. (Russians)	13	2.5	5	6600	Brook trout
Horse Range Lk. (Marbles)	7	3.5	8	6000	Grass and brush shore, brook trout
Horseshoe Lk.	13	6	21	6400	Brook and rainbow trout
Independence Lk	9	1.5	10	5950	Wooded shore, lily pads; brook trout
Josephine Lk.	13	2	10	7350	Many brook trout
Katherine Lk.	7	5	13	5800	Wooded, level shore; brook and rainbow
Kidder Lk.	6	2	15	5900	Meadowed shore, rainbow
Kleaver Lk.	6	2.5	17	6450	Steep, wooded, brushy shore; brook trout
Lk. of the Island	7	13	25	5650	Open, somewhat brushy shore; brook and rainbow
Lipstick Lk.	13	1.5	9	6350	Brook trout
Log Lk.	5	1	15	5400	Wooded shore, many logs, brook trout
Long High Lk.	5	1.5	6	7150	Grassy shore, brook trout
Lost Lk.	7	8	30	5650	Brushy, wooded shore; brook, rainbow and brown trout
Maneaten Lk.	6	14	112	6200	Very steep, rocky shore; rainbow trout
Marten Lk.	6	1	10	6350	Brushy, rock ledge shore; brook and rainbow
McCash Lk.	9	3.5	3	5400	Wooded, brushy shore; a few rainbow
Meteor Lk.	9	3.5	11	5700	Grassy, wooded shore; rainbow
Meeks Meadow Lk.	16	2	10	6150	Meadowed shore, many brook trout

LAKE	Chapt	Acres	Depth	Elev.	COMMENTS
Milne Lk.	6	2.5	39	6750	Rocky shore, brook and rainbow
Monument Lk	9	3	13	5900	Meadowed shore, brook and rainbow
Onemile Lk.	9	22	32	5750	Varied shore, brook and rainbow
Paradise Lk	2	5	15	6200	Grassy shore, brook trout
Paynes Lk.	12	16	50	6450	Mostly open shore, brook and rainbow
Pine Lk.	7	3.5	20	6300	Wooded shore, brook and rainbow
Pleasant Lk.	9	9	37	5550	Steep, rocky, wooded shore; brook trout
Rainy Lk.	3	5.5	18	5400	Brushy shore, brook trout
Lower Ruffey Lk	16	1.5	4	6050	Good brook trout
U. Ruffey Lk.	16	2.5	8	6400	Brook trout
Russian Lk.	15	5	72	7100	Rocky shore, rainbow trout
Golden Russian Lk.	15	1.5	8	6080	Rock ledge shore, possibly golden trout
Lower Russian Lk.	15	2	12	6500	Meadowed shore, brook trout, natural repro
Secret Lk.	9	8.5	43	5250	Brush and large rocks at shore, brook and rainbow
Shadow Lk.	3	2.5	14	6450	Woods and grass shore, brook and rainbow
Shelly Lk.	6	5.5	43	6700	Level, rocky shore; brook and rainbow
Siphon Lk.	15	1.5	22	7250	Rainbow trout
Lower Sky High Lk.	3	12.5	56	6000	Open shore; rainbow, brook, brown
U. Sky High Lk.	3	4	38	6000	Open shore; brook and brown
Smith Lk.	16	6	56	6950	Brook, rainbow, brown trout
Snyder Lk	9	2.5	47	5800	Very steep, rocky shore; rainbow
Spirit Lk	3	3.5	41	5950	Steep, brushy shore; brook trout
Statue Lk.	16	1	15	7200	Rocky shore, brook trout
Steinacher Lk.	7	2.5	5	5800	Level basin; open, grassy shore; brook and rainbow
S. Sugar Lk.	14	3.5	??	6850	Rocky shore, rainbow trout
Summit Lk.	5	5	15	6050	Woods and meadow shore, brook trout
Summit Meadow Lk.	5	1.5	4	6050	Meadowed shore, brook trout
Taylor Lk.	11	12	35	6500	Mostly wooded shore, brook trout
Tickner Lk.	9	1.5	9	6300	Open shore, brook trout
Tom's Lk. (near Spirit Lk.)	3	4	10	5200	Level, brush and grass shore; brook and rainbow
Twin Lk.	11	1	15	6700	Brook trout, natural repro

LAKE	Chapt	Acres	Depth	Elev.	COMMENTS
Ukonom Lk.	9	67	68	6050	Varied, mostly open shore, brook and rainbow
Waterdog Lk.	15	3.5	16	7000	Wooded shore, brook and rainbow
Wild Lk	7	3.5	24	5400	Brushy shore, brook and rainbow
Wolverine Lk.	4	1.5	11	7000	Open, level shore; brook trout
Wooley Lk.	6	6.5	84	6700	Very steep, open, rocky shore; rainbow trout
Lower Wright Lk	4	26	90	6900	Open shore; brook, rainbow, brown
U. Wright Lk.	4	6.5	50	7400	Wooded shore; brook trout

Acknowledgments and bibliography

This book would not be nearly as thorough or interesting without the assistance of a number of individuals and resources. Above all, I acknowledge the patience and helpfulness of the staff of the USDA Forest Service. Among their many employees I've pestered over the years, Chuck Smith, of the Scott River Ranger District, stands out as a knowledgeable friend with a deep sense of the poetry contained in the areas under his jurisdiction (although he'd likely punch me for making such an allegation). Marla Knight, Doug Andrews, Dave Algren, Pat Garrihan, Julie Knorr, Barbara Williams, Mike Lee and Al Molitor also contributed.

I would also like to thank Brian Boothby, an enthusiastic companion on a number of these excursions, Gilberto d'Urso, my publisher at Mountain N'Air Books, John Erwin, and my wife, Patricia.

Finally, I confess to having consulted a number of references in finalizing the material herein, including the works of those who preceded me in writing about the Marble Mountains. I cite the following:

Bernstein, Art, "Best Day-Hikes of the California Northwest," (Mountain N'Air Books, 1991).

Bernstein, Art, "Best Hikes of the Trinity Alps," (Mountain N'Air Books, 1992).

Bernstein, Art, "Native Trees of the Northwest," (Magnifica Books, 1988).

Green, David, "Marble Mountain Wilderness," (Wilderness Press, 1980).

Lowe, Don and Roberta, "41 Northwest California Hiking Trails," (Touchstone Press, 1981).

Niehaus, T.F., and Ripper, C.L., "Peterson's Field Guide to Pacific States Wildflowers." (Houghton Mifflin, 1976)

Schaffer, Jeff, et al, "The Pacific Crest Trail, Vol. 1: California," (Wilderness Press, 1990).

On footnotes and egos

Finally, I must tell the story about the time I was reading a newly published book on the natural history of the area where I live. At one point, the author made a statement which I found extremely fascinating.

"That's interesting," I said to myself. "I wonder where she heard about it?"

My question was quickly answered by a reference citation at the end of the paragraph. It referred to a book I'd written.

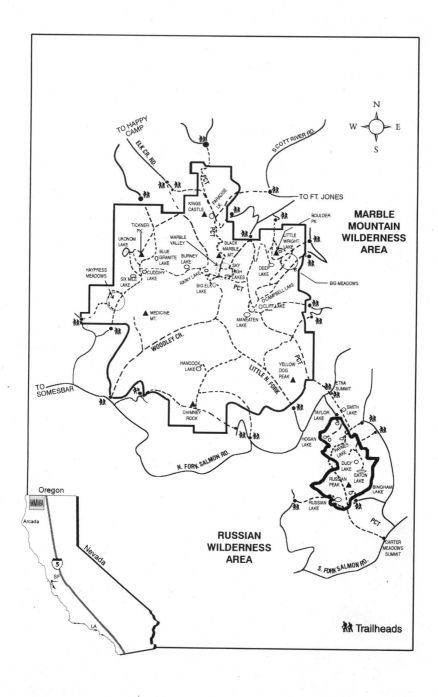

THE MARBLE MOUNTAIN WILDERNESS AREA

Photo by Art Bernstein

1. KELSEY TRAIL/MAPLE FALLS

Destinations:	Fish Camp, Maple Falls
Length:	4 miles (Maple Falls)
Water:	Yes, plentiful
Season:	Any
Difficulty:	Moderate
Elevation:	2400 to 4300 feet
USGS 7.5 topo:	Grider Valley
Location:	T44N-R11W-Sector 21
Use:	Non-motorized only
Use intensity:	Moderate
Camping:	Bridge Flat CG
Ownership:	Klamath National Forest
Phone:	(916) 468-5351

Directions: Take I-5 to south Yreka and follow Highway-3 to Fort Jones, turning right onto the Scott River Road. Past the Kelsey Guard Station and just before Bridge Flat, the blacktop crosses the Scott River. Turn left on the dirt road immediately over the bridge. Do not cross a second bridge, ½ mile up, but continue straight, past the house, to the roomy trailhead. The last few hundred feet are not as bad as they look. There are no signs until you reach the trailhead, because of private property.

The trail can also be reached from Bridge Flat Campground. Hike up an unmarked skid road across the road and look for a small sign pointing left. Add a mile if you begin here.

March to the Marbles: The Kelsey Trail

The Kelsey Trail was built by the Army over 150 years ago. Fort Jones was an actual fort then and the area was gripped in a gold rush. Despite some extremely rugged country and a couple of high passes, the route served as a main supply line from Crescent City until the turn of the century.

Elsewhere in the Marbles, the seven mile Bear Creek Trail to Bear Lake, from Sulphur Springs (Chapter 2), also follows the Kelsey Trail. Across the Klamath, in the Siskiyou Wilderness, the spectacular route to a different Bear Lake, near Clear Creek, and the path along the Smith River's South Fork, are both segments of the same Kelsey Trail. All are well worth visiting.

While winter is the most interesting time to tour the Kelsey Trail's low elevation Maple Falls segment, you may not make it to Maple Falls because of snow. In mid-summer, the canyon tends to heat up, also due to low elevation. I'd suggest spring, when the sweet pea, scarlet fritillary, delphinium and Indian paintbrush are in bloom.

The only constant on this exciting and remarkably varied pathway, is the crash of whitewater, as the creek surges through a narrow gorge, often hemmed by sheer, moss-and-fern rock walls. The trail alternates between gentle woods, visits to the water's edge to peek at waterfalls or alder flats; and exposed cliffs and rock points hundreds of feet above the water.

In my December, 1988 visit, I counted eight side creeks in the three miles to the spot where I was turned back by snow, just beyond the Wilderness boundary. Some charged down black gorges which never saw the light of day. Some were wide, airy and boulder strewn. Some fanned out over glistening black rock faces while others dropped in stairstep pools and ledges. At least one entailed fording knee deep water. A couple streams on the opposite side plunged 1000 feet before meeting the creek.

In my May, 1994 visit, I encountered only two flowing streams. The formerly knee deep one was barely a trickle.

Despite an average rise of 500 feet per mile, the trail contains long, level stretches, with much of its elevation gain confined to short pitches and the final mile. Forests are mainly middle elevation, consisting of Douglas-fir, white fir, black oak, white oak, madrone, ponderosa pine and sugar pine. Abundant canyon liveoak indicates thin soils, low elevations and steep slopes.

Watch for signs of repeated fires, the worst being in 1987 and 1991. Devastation from the 1987 burn can be seen along the ridgetops and across the canyon at Maple Falls. Around the trail, damage was light. Many conifers survived, despite being charred at the base. Most hardwoods did not, although some madrone and liveoak skeletons have resprouted.

A quarter-mile from the trailhead, the path picks up an old ditch for ⅛ mile, which was originally intended to carry water to hydraulic gold miners at Scott Bar, but was never competed. Water from the ditch was later used to turn Pelton wheels to provide electricity for a CCC camp, local residences and a small sawmill.

Hydraulic mining is a process where potentially gold bearing soil is washed from the hillside through a sluice by a giant hose. Rusted metal half-pipes, a former continuation of the ditch, are piled alongside the trail. The ditch originates at a large alder flat with an immense landslide on the opposite hillside.

Two miles up, the trail drops near the creek, climbs some steep switchbacks, then makes a large "U" across a second creek. Just before the switchbacks, a 30 foot waterfall surges through a narrow, vertical walled chasm. A short way trail leads to the falls and adjacent Fish Camp. Look for a makeshift wooden picnic table. Fish Camp offers a beautiful, easy winter destination.

The Wilderness boundary lies ½ mile beyond Fish Camp, atop a second, shorter series of switchbacks. Soon after, the trail enters a large side creek, opposite a nearly vertical north slope. Heretofore, the path has followed a sunny south slope. Where the trail ascends the short but steep north pitch, my December visit ended. A single patch of snow was too steep to traverse and I saw no reasonable way around.

Beyond the crossing, the path cuts south as it makes its way into the quiet canyon of the Kelsey Creek North Fork. It soon crosses the North fork, doubles back for a considerable distance at a steep incline, then reenters the noisy and spectacular main canyon, hundreds of feet above the water. The final mile to Maple Falls rises 700 feet.

The initial glimpse of the falls comes ½ mile after the North Fork crossing. Then it's back into the woods, amid much huffing and puffing and several side streams.

Maple Falls, easily visible from the trail, plunges 50 feet in a split flow, with braided cascades above and below. A side trail leads to a lovely flat just above the falls. While most of the trees are cedar and alder, there are enough bigleaf maples to justify the name.

I suggest Maple Falls as a day-hike turnaround. A steep, rocky mile beyond, the gorge widens somewhat to a meadowed valley. Although not visible along most of the path, Kings Castle, a 7400 foot marble outcropping, towers above the head of Kelsey Creek. Paradise Lake (Chapter 2), nestles at 6100 feet, at the foot of Kings Castle, three miles and 1800 feet above Maple Falls, and seven miles from the trailhead. The difficult Paradise Lake Trail, from the end of the Canyon Creek/Lover's Camp Road, reaches Paradise Lake in two miles.

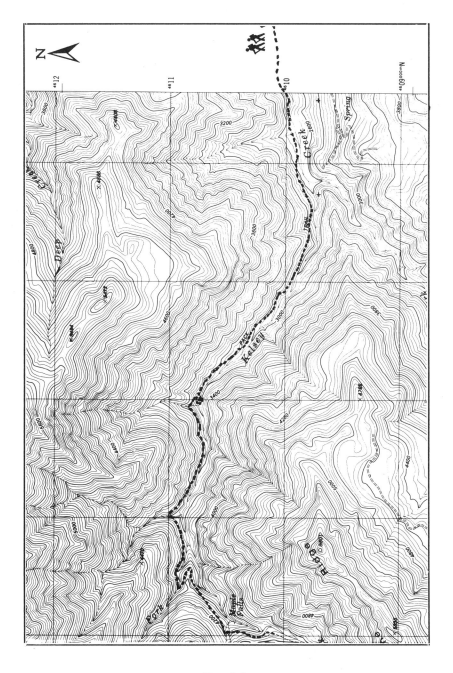

Map 1.1

2.

Destinations:	Paradise Lake, Turk Lake, Bear Lake, *Pacific Crest Trail*
Length:	2 miles (Paradise Lake)
	3 miles (Bear Lake)
Water:	OK
Season:	June through October
Difficulty:	Difficult
Elevation:	4800 to 6200 feet
USGS 7.5" topo:	Grider Valley, Marble Mountain
Location:	T44N-R12W-Sector 36
Use:	Non-motorized only
Use intensity:	Moderate
Camping:	Indian Scotty
Ownership:	Klamath National Forest
Phone:	(916) 468-5351

Directions: Take I-5 to the south Yreka (Hwy 3) exit. Proceed to Fort Jones. Turn right onto the Scott River Road and follow it to the Indian Scotty Bridge. Cross the bridge and follow Canyon Creek Road (44N45), past the Lovers Camp turnoff to the Paradise Lake trailhead. The route is well signed

Paradise

While not the highest peak in the Marble Mountains, Kings Castle, at 7400 feet, is among the most significant. It used to be called Marble Mountain and the Wilderness was named for it. The name was later changed to avoid confusion with the Marble Rim and Black Marble Mountain. Kings Castle is an appropriate name for an exquisite slice of scenery.

In 1970, the shortest route to Paradise Lake was the seven mile Kelsey Trail from Bridge Flat on the Scott River (Chapter 1). Logging roads have since pushed into the Canyon Creek drainage to within two miles of the lake. These highly scenic roads offer peeks into the Marble Valley area and close-up looks at Kings Castle. A brief view of Kings Castle also appears from the Scott River Road. Look for a white outcropping resembling a giant loaf of bread, perched atop a green mountain.

Canyon Creek Road is wide and well groomed. The last couple miles to the trailhead follow a spur which is much narrower and a little rougher. A quarter-mile before the trailhead, the road fords the South Fork of Kelsey Creek. You may wish to park there if water is high.

Though quite steep, the path can be negotiated in an hour or so. After winding breathlessly, and seemingly endlessly, back and forth up a densely wooded slope, it breaks onto a brushy ridge surrounded by giant cliffs. Canyon Creek, the Marble Rim and the Scott River Canyon can be seen in the distance.

Immediately after, the trail enters a meadowed basin decorated with clumps of red fir and mountain hemlock. The shallow, five acre, green water lake adorns its center. It is stocked with brook trout. The lake's deepest spot (15 feet), nestles against a low rock face below a vast green slope. The Kings Castle outcropping crowns the top of the slope. Another outcropping, to the left, is much larger but not as pretty.

The Paradise Lake Trail joins the Pacific Crest Trail at the entrance to the basin, just before the lake. A left on the PCT (Chapter 10), will land you in Marble Valley (Chapter 3), via scenic Big Rock Valley and Black Marble Mountain. This route to Marble Valley is rapidly gaining popularity, reaching it in seven miles from the trailhead, versus four. And in answer to your question, yes, this really is Paradise. No fooling.

North from Paradise: Turk and Bear Lakes

Two large ponds, Turk and Bear Lake, lie within two miles of Paradise Lake. Both are reached by hiking north for 1½ miles on the PCT as it ascends the barren Kings Castle Ridge, rising from 6100 feet foot saddle. At the saddle, look for a side trail on the right for Turk Lake and one on the left for Bear Lake.

Occupying an open, rocky basin, ½ mile and 800 feet below the PCT, Turk Lake covers two acres and is unstocked. 800 feet in ½ mile, in case you didn't know it, is exceedingly steep. Turk Lake can also be reached via a cutoff on the Kelsey Trail, two miles above Maple Falls.

Bear Lake is considerably more attractive than Turk Lake. It sits in the center of a small, steep, treeless basin at the base of a 500 foot cliff, between the Kings Castle Ridge and the convoluted, red serpentine outcropping of Red Rock Mountain. The Bear Lake access trail isn't quite as steep as Turk Lake's, dropping "only" 600 feet in ½ mile from the saddle. The shallow, two acre, extremely rocky lake is stocked with brook trout.

Bear Lake is also reached via the Bear Creek segment of the Kelsey Trail, a seven mile hike from Sulphur Springs Campground, out of Happy Camp. You can knock 2½ miles off this route by following road 15N06, from just before Sulphur Springs to where it dead ends at Snowshoe Creek. There's a great waterfall between the lower and upper trailheads. The initial mile from the upper trailhead climbs 1200 feet, after which the path levels considerably.

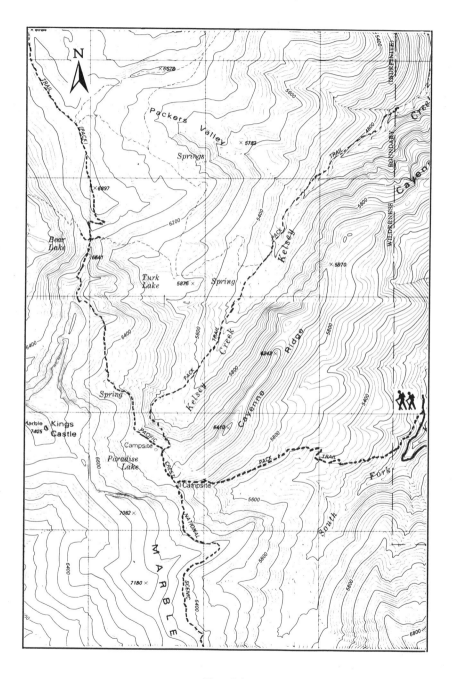

Map 2.1

3. MARBLE VALLEY/SKY HIGH/ RED ROCK/RAINY VALLEY

Destinations:	Marble Valley, Little Marble Valley, Sky High Lakes, Marble Rim, Marble Gap, Big Elk Lake, Rainy Lake, Rainy Valley, Spirit Lake, Tom's Lake, Burney Lake, Shadow Lake, Red Rock Valley, Little Elk Lake, Big Rock Valley, Box Camp Ridge, Pacific Crest Trail.
Length:	4½ miles (Marble Valley)
	6 miles (Sky High Lakes)
	6 miles (Marble Gap)
	7 miles (Big Elk Lake)
	6½ miles (Marble Rim overlook)
	10 miles (Rainy Lake)
	13 miles (Burney Lake)
Water:	OK
Season:	June through October
Difficulty:	Moderate
Elevation:	4300 to 5900 feet (Marble Valley)
	6200 feet (Four Corners Saddle)
	6700 feet (Marble Rim Trail)
	6800 feet (Marble Gap)
	5700 feet (Sky High Valley)
	4700 feet (Rainy Valley)
	5400 feet (Rainy Lake)
	6000 feet (Big Elk Lake)
	5200 feet (Red Rock Valley cabin)
	5900 feet (Red Rock/Little Elk Lake crest)
	5300 feer (Little Elk Lake)
USGS 7.5" topo:	Marble Mountain

Location:	T43N-R11W-Sector 8
Use:	Non-motorized only
Use intensity:	Very Heavy
Camping:	Indian Scotty, Lovers Camp
Ownership:	Klamath National Forest
Phone:	(916) 468-5351

Directions: Leave I-5 at the Highway-3 (south Yreka) exit. Follow Highway-3 to Fort Jones and turn right onto the blacktopped Scott River Road. Proceed to the Indian Scotty Bridge. Cross the bridge onto the wide gravel road and follow the signs to the giant Lovers Camp trailhead complex and campground.

Marble Valley: The most beautiful place I've ever been

On my first Marble Valley visit, in 1970, it became ingrained in my memory as the most beautiful place I'd ever been. When I visited it the second time, in 1994, having devoted much of my life to seeking out nationally renowned scenic wonders, I found it 10 times more beautiful than I remembered. I consider Marble Valley, at the very least, the ultimate journey into the glacial valleys of the Klamath Mountains system.

A word of caution. The Canyon Creek Trail from Lovers Camp is extremely popular. If you visit on a July weekend, be prepared for a procession of horses, pack animals, Boy Scouts, etc. They can raise much dust. Many hikers reach Marble Valley via the Paradise Lake (Chapter 2) or Box Camp Trails. While this adds a couple miles, the crowds are much less and the trailhead is 600 feet higher.

The Lovers Camp trailhead complex accommodates 100 cars and horse trailers. From the horse trailhead, the path follows a gated road for ¼ mile. From the hiker trailhead, the route runs through a grassy field into the woods for ¼ mile, before meeting the closed road from the horse trailhead. The actual Canyon Creek Trail begins where the horse and hiker paths join.

The Canyon Creek Trail's initial three miles are remarkably level. The creek flows through a wide, densely forested valley, with the path high up the hillside. While water abounds most of the time, when I visited in August of an unusually dry year, the only water came at Death Valley Creek (ironically), and at the Canyon Creek crossing just below Marble Valley.

Despite generally level ground, the route's first three miles transition from low elevation Douglas-fir, sugar pine, white fir, ponderosa pine, oak and madrone forests to higher elevation stands of white pine and red fir, with mountain hemlock in the highest areas. Look for much Sadler oak in the understory. The somewhat rare shrub is indigenous only to the Klamath mountains.

Three miles up, just beyond a swath-like opening on the right with a brief view of Black Marble Mountain, the path abruptly steepens, gaining 1200 feet in 1½ miles. A highlight is the crossing of Canyon Creek, at a rock ledge with multi-tiered cascades above and below.

Shortly beyond the creek crossing, the lower trail to Sky High Lakes peels off left. If that's where you're headed, this is your turnoff. If going to Marble Valley prior to Sky High Lakes, use the second Sky High Lakes turnoff, ½ mile up. You can also loop into the Sky High basin from Four Corners Saddle, located a mile beyond Marble Valley.

Four and a half miles from Lovers Camp, the Marble Valley suddenly unfolds in front of you. It may take a while to soak in the exquisite beauty. Side trails abound so bring a map and do some exploring. Immediately west of Marble Valley, and totally overwhelming it, rises a 500 to 1000 foot thick band of snowy white marble, called the Marble Rim or simply Marble Mountain. Kings Castle Mountain, four miles north, is also sometimes called Marble Mountain. The outcropping of brown schist capping the Marble Rim's north end is incorrectly named Black Marble Mountain.

The Marble Valley side of the Marble Rim is a gently sloping expanse. The other side has been deeply gouged into a series of steep walled glacial cirques above Rainy and Elk Creek Valleys. The best place to view Rainy Valley is the Marble Rim Trail, which begins at Four Corners Saddle, a mile south on the PCT. The Marble Gap Trail, ¼ mile north of Marble Valley, also offers a sweeping view of Rainy Valley, plus a panorama of the entire Marble Valley area. Try to get a look at both sides of the rim.

The National Speleological Society's Portland Grotto has mapped over 80 caves within the Marble Rim, all containing stalactites and other flowstone formations. The biggest, Bigfoot Cave, is larger than the cave at Oregon Caves National Monument. It was only discovered in 1976.

Most cave openings are marked by vertical drops and are very dangerous. Also, dripstone formations inside are extremely fragile and take hundreds of thousands of years to form. The Forest Service and Speleological Society ask that only serious cavers visit these sites. For information, contact the NSP's Portland Grotto, Mount Shasta Grotto or a Yreka Group called the Klamath Mountains Conservation Task Force.

Marble Valley itself is a small grassy flat with a couple cabins. Creeks on either side, choked with willow and alder brush, normally provide plenty of water, although both were dry in my 1994 visits. The Canyon Creek Trail ends in the middle of the flat, at the junction with the PCT. Head south (left) for Four Corners Saddle, Big Elk Lake, the Marble Rim Trail, Red Rock Valley and the Wilderness core. Go north (right), for the Box Camp Trail, Paradise Lake and the Marble Gap Trail.

Little Marble Valley, down the PCT to the left, is even prettier than Marble Valley. It consists of a spot where the marble extends across the valley floor. Profuse wildflowers sprout between cracks in the marble tile.

I suggest Marble Valley, Sky High Lakes, the crest of the Marble Gap Trail and/or the Marble Rim Trail overlook, as the limits of a day hike. For other destinations, figure on at least spending the night.

Above Marble Valley: Four Corners, Marble Rim Trail

A mile past Marble Valley, the PCT emerges at a 6200 foot ridge called, "Four Corners Saddle." From there, a left turn takes you on the PCT to Sky High Valley via the cliff tops, then to Red Rock Valley, Shackleford Creek and Mexico. Go straight at the saddle and you'll drop down to Big Elk Lake and the upper end of the Wooley Creek Trail, before continuing on to Rainy, Burney and the Cuddihy Lakes. The latter lies 16 miles from Lovers Camp. A right turn onto the Marble Rim Trail, from the saddle, bypasses Big Elk Lake and offers incredible views of Rainy Valley and Big Elk Lake, before rejoining the Cuddihy Lake Trail two miles west.

The view from Four Corners Saddle is mind boggling. The Marble Rim dominates, just as it dominates most vista points for 50 miles in every direction. South of the saddle, the entire Wooley Creek drainage can be seen, dropping from 6200 feet where you're standing, to 640 feet at the creek mouth, 25 miles away (Chapter 8). The craggy jumble to the southeast is the peaks around Shackleford Creek and Maneaten Lake. They're just as impressive close up (Chapter 5).

In 1970, there was no Marble Rim Trail. My recollection is that on arriving at the saddle, I lit out across the marble to the crest of the rim. I don't remember it being that difficult, although from the look of things in 1994, my trek entailed a mile cross country, with a 600 foot rise. Photos verify that I did indeed make it.

The Marble Rim Trail, alas, does not traverse the actual Marble Rim. It rises steeply, to 6700 feet, on the flank of the non-marble cap rock forming the rim's south end. The emerging view of the forests, meadows and headwalls of the Big Elk Lake basin, a few hundred feet below, is outstanding, especially after the lake finally comes into view.

The Marble Rim Trail's highlight is a gap shortly beyond the crest, with a remarkable view into Rainy Valley. Consider this: (1) The elevation at Rainy Valley is 4700 feet. (2) The Marble Rim elevation is 6800 to 7400 feet. (3) Most of the dropoff is absolutely or nearly vertical. (4) The cliffs continue similarly around three sides of the valley head. (5) Elk Valley, one basin north on the west side of Black Marble Mountain (7400 feet), is even more impressive. It is visited by the Rainy Gap Trail from Marble Valley.

Rainy Lake occupies a pocket on the northwest end of Rainy Valley, at 5400 feet. To see it, you'll have to hike three miles beyond the Marble Rim Trail overlook.

By heading east on the PCT from Four Corners Saddle, a loop can be made back into Sky High Lakes, via the top of the encircling cliffs. For a peek at the lakes from a ledge near the cliff top, you only need to walk ¾ mile from Four Corners Saddle. This is not a bad option, especially on a day hike. As beautiful as the lakes are up close, they're even prettier from above.

Scenery and people: The Sky High Lakes

Of the hundreds of glacial cirque lakes in the Marbles and Trinity Alps, these rank among the prettiest. Nestled at the foot of a soaring, circular black schist headwall, the phrase "emerald necklace" comes to mind in describing the three lake chain. The cliffs stand in gorgeous contrast to the rolling, golden meadows of the valley floor.

From Canyon Creek, you enter the valley at ½ acre Gate Lake, which is 12 feet deep and stocked with rainbow and brook trout. Gate Lake is a mile from the Canyon Creek Trail's upper turnoff, a mile from Lower Sky High Lake and five miles from Lover's Camp.

After one more mile, rising gently through grass, corn lily meadows, creeks, wildflowers and aspen groves, you arrive at Lower Sky High Lake. Look behind you, at the top of the rise near the aspen groves, just before the lake, for one of the better views of the Marble Rim.

Lower Sky High Lake covers 12 acres at 6000 feet elevation. It reaches a depth of 56 feet and contains rainbow, brook and brown trout. Upper Sky High Lake is separated from it by a mass of willow and alder brush. Brook and rainbow trout lurk in the upper lake's four acre, 38 feet deep waters. Frying Pan Lake lies five minutes above the upper lake, away from the cliffs. It covers two acres and is unstocked. And yes, Frying Pan Lake is shaped like a frying pan, with a long, narrow projection jutting from one end. It has also been called Banjo Lake.

Judiciously placed clumps of hemlock, white pine and red fir add to the basin's beauty and provide numerous sheltered campsites. There is a log shelter near the lower lake outlet. If you camp here, bear in mind that the area is extremely popular and that even low noises carry an amazing distance. Try Shadow Lake for a more secluded alternative.

The Sky High basin was one of the few places which made me wish I knew more about bird identification. I saw dozens of songbirds. I also observed a northern goshawk (possibly) and a rufous sided hummingbird. There were remarkably few insects.

Beyond Frying Pan Lake, the path begins a serious climb, over a series of meadowed benches and ledges, to the encircling 6600 foot rim. It offers some great vistas of the valley. From the crest above the basin, it's only ¾ mile back to Four Corners Saddle.

The long way home:
Shadow Lake, Red Rock Valley, Little Elk Lake

At Four Corners Saddle, the PCT makes a 90 degree turn east, climbing gently. It's ¼ mile to the high trail into Sky High Lakes. Follow the upper end of the Sky High Lakes Trail, off the PCT, for ½ mile to an excellent vista point. If you remain on the PCT, you'll soon hit the top of the Sky High Valley's south rim, with another outstanding view.

Soon after, still gently climbing, the PCT swings away from the ridge top and around a small outcropping. Look for a steep, rocky, ¼ mile side trail to the mostly forested shore of Shadow Lake, a 2½ acre, 14 foot deep pool stocked with brook trout. Shadow Lake is perched high up in the metavolcanic crags directly overlooking Lower Sky High Lake. The view is impressive.

Two Miles on the PCT from Four Corners Saddle, the Red Rock Valley Trail takes off left. It makes a wonderful alternate route back to Lovers Camp, for a 13 mile loop. It also offers an impressive, fairly easy day-hike from Lover's Camp. Since Red Rock Valley's most scenic portions lie 1000 feet lower than those of Marble Valley, it is accessible sooner and offers a outstanding early season opportunities. It's 5 miles from Lover's Camp to the PCT/Red Rock Valley junction and 3½ miles from Lover's Camp to Little Elk Lake.

From its upper end, Red Rock Valley Trail drops steeply down a small cirque headwall, past a large pond. The valley is named for the barren, unnamed, 7600 foot peak of orange serpentinite which rises straight up from the creek's east shore. In the upper canyon, Boulder Peak, highest in the Wilderness, is visible behind the unnamed peak. Most of the canyon is lined with cascading side creeks, waterfalls along the main creek and vast meadows of grass, boulders, corn lily to the west. There are also many cows. Higher up the canyon, groves of quaking aspen cover the meadows, with closely related and similar appearing black cottonwoods along the creek (along with mountain hemlock, Western white pine, white fir and Sadler oak). Since aspen reproduces through cloning via root runners, every tree in a stand has interconnected roots and is genetically identical to every other tree.

Working your way downstream, the conifer forest gradually closes in. Eventually, the path passes a last meadow with a cabin, then swings west, contouring gradually around the hillside and dropping down to Canyon Creek in a series of long switchbacks. After crossing Canyon Creek, the path joins the Canyon Creek Trail ½ mile from Lovers Camp. The Canyon Creek crossing is via an immense fallen log, which is crucial in early season when the creek's rushing water may be neck deep. Getting on and off the log requires a little work but the log itself is huge and very stable. Later in the season, the creek settles down to about ankle depth.

Two miles down the Red Rock Valley Trail, the path to Little Elk Lake comes in on the right (east), near an excellent campsite in a small meadow. When I visited Red Rock Valley in early June of a very wet year, the creek was very fast, knee deep and extremely foreboding. I didn't cross it. The Little Elk Lake Trail is a killer route, rising 700 feet in a mile, then dropping 600 feet in the same distance. Little Elk Lake is a handsome pool, set amid metavolcanic pinnacles rising from a brush and meadow shore. The six acre lake is only five feet deep and very muddy, with an elevation of 5400 feet. It contains a naturally reproducing population of rainbow and brown trout.

The oddest thing about Little Elk Lake is that it is bigger than Big Elk Lake. Big Elk Lake lies seven miles distant and 1½ miles from Four Corners Saddle.

Should you continue on the Little Elk Lake Trail, you'll end up at Deep Lake in 3½ miles. One of the lovelier lakes in the Wilderness, Deep Lake lies eight miles from Lover's Camp and six miles from the Boulder Creek trailhead (Chapter 4). Because the Boulder Creek Trail rises 3000 feet in its first three miles, most people visit via Lover's Camp, even though I included it in the Boulder Creek Chapter. I like the Boulder Creek Trail.

Into the Wilderness: Big Elk Lake, Rainy Lake, Burney Lake

The cross-wilderness trail, heading west from Four Corners Saddle, visits a number of remote lakes, starting with Big Elk and Rainy

Lakes. It is 1½ miles to Big Elk Lake from the saddle, on a trail which drops 800 feet, then rises 600 feet. You'll add a mile but save much climbing by heading out the Marble Rim Trail and approaching Big Elk Lake from the opposite direction. The 4½ acre, 10 foot deep, green water lake, surrounded by meadows and a gentle headwall, is stocked with brook and rainbow trout.

Of all the lakes in the Marbles, Big Elk is the only one set in a marble basin. Glacial basins carved in marble normally do not form lakes because marble is so porous. In this case, the lake itself is in a different rock type than the headwall.

Beyond Big Elk Lake, the path climbs 300 feet, steeply at first then leveling off. It joins the far end of the Marble Rim Trail a mile past the lake. The Rainy Lake turnoff shows up 1½ miles later.

The best way to reach Rainy Lake is via the Marble Rim Trail, which is shorter and much easier than the Big Elk Lake route. Two miles from Four Corners Saddle, the Marble Rim Trail dives over a ridge into a wooded basin, dropping 400 feet in ¼ mile. After rejoining the trail from Big Elk Lake, it levels off as it contours around the North Fork of Wooley Creek.

The ¾ mile spur into Rainy Lake plunges another 600 feet, for a drop of 1300 feet from the Marble Rim Trail's high point. Considering the ups and downs, the excessive mileage, and a rather mediocre destination, Rainy Lake is surprisingly popular. In contrast to Rainy Valley's awesome splendor, the lake is disappointing, with a brushy shore and obscured views of the surrounding cliffs. The 5400 foot elevation lake covers 5½ acres, is 18 feet deep and contains brook trout. There are several excellent campsites at the lake.

Rainy Lake can also be reached via the Rainy Gap Trail from Marble Valley, discussed later, and the Rainy Valley Trail from Sulphur Springs, up densely forested Elk Creek, out of Happy Camp. Via Sulphur Springs, it's 10 miles to Rainy Lake, the same as via the Canyon Creek/Marble Rim Trails. Via Canyon Creek and the horrendously steep Marble Gap Trail, it's eight miles.

A mile beyond the Rainy Lake turnoff, on the way west to Cuddihy Lakes, the trail hits a ridge top, which it straddles for ½ mile. Tom's Lake lies ½ mile and 800 feet below the wooded headwall north of the ridge, at the western base of Elk Peak, highest in the vicinity at 7000 feet. The lake covers four acres, at 5200 feet elevation. It is 10 feet deep and contains brook and rainbow trout. There is no trail to it.

Just beyond the saddle above Tom's Lake, the cross-wilderness trail passes Spirit Lake, nestled in a tiny basin alongside the trail. The lake covers 3½ acres at 6000 feet, is deep for its size at 41 feet and contains rainbow trout. The shore is quite brushy but several fine campsites hide back in the woods.

The Burney Lake turnoff shows up 1½ miles beyond Spirit Lake, at a place called Pigeon's Roost, an open, rocky pinnacle dotted with picturesque tree clumps. Approaching Pigeon's Roost, look behind you for a view of the west side of Elk Peak, the massive rock pyramid anchoring Rainy Valley's western wall. Watch for a grove of knobcone pine just beyond Pigeon's Roost.

Like Tom's Lake, Burney Lake lies a half-mile away and 700 feet down. Unlike Tom's Lake, Burney Lake boasts an access trail, although it is faint and bone-jarringly steep. Unlike most lakes in this chapter, Burney is quite substantial, covering 15 acres and reaching a depth of 25 feet. A naturally producing brook trout population, and a lovely woods and meadow shore, entice a surprising number of anglers. A large campsite enhance the beauty of the level, wooded east shore.

Burney Lake's main drawback is its remoteness. Within the Wilderness, only Hancock Lake (Chapter 7), may be more difficult to reach. It's 13 miles to Burney Lake via Lovers Camp and 12 to 14 via Sulphur Springs. West of the Burney Lake turnoff, it's only two miles to the Cuddihy Lakes access trail. That's discussed in Chapter 9.

Spectacular longcuts: The Marble Gap and Box Camp Trails

The trek north on the PCT from Marble Valley, towards Paradise Lake, yields a number of surprises. The first, ¼ mile away, requires some explanation: The Marble Rim is actually two rims, divided by a 6800 foot, non-marble gap directly above Marble Valley. The Marble Gap Trail to Rainy Valley utilizes this break spectacularly.

Although the Marble Gap Trail reaches Rainy Lake in 3½ miles, it is no shortcut. From the PCT junction, this breathtaking (literally) path rises 900 feet in a mile, to 6800 feet. It winds through a series of meadows and outcroppings, each steeper than the last and all surrounded by vast marble walls. The final approach to the gap ranks among the steepest trail pitches I've been on.

The route crests at the base of the immense marble cliff to your left (south). While the Marble Rim Trail offers a slightly better perspective of Rainy Valley, there is no better panorama of the Marble Valley than the top of the gap trail. Not only can the entire valley be seen, so can much of the Sky High Valley (you can't quite see the lakes), Red Rock Valley, Deep Lake Valley and Boulder Peak, highest in the Marbles at 8299 feet. To the west, beyond Rainy Valley, the entire Western Siskiyous, a 7300 foot range between the Klamath River and the ocean, is visible. In between lies the bulk of the Wilderness, highlighted by Elk Peak and Medicine Mountain.

Beyond the gap, the trail careens dizzyingly into Rainy Valley, bottoming out after two more miles and a drop of 2000 feet. On the way, it brushes the barren ridge between Rainy Valley and Elk Valley. After crossing Rainy Creek amid a towering, old growth jungle crawling with bigfeet and leprechauns, the last mile to Rainy Lake climbs 600 feet.

North on the PCT, past the Marble Gap junction, it is $2\frac{1}{2}$ miles to the upper end of the Box Camp Trail. This is a lovely segment which crosses the infant Canyon Creek, then makes its way around a point, just below Black Marble Mountain. Look for some small cave openings where the trail breaks out of the woods at a white marble band on Black Marble Mountain's northeast side.

The top of Black Marble Mountain is actually brown schist, with white marble underneath. Marble and schist are metamorphic rocks which have been chemically altered over great time periods. Marble is metamorphosed limestone, a marine sediment. Most schist is metamorphosed lava. The metavolcanic rock underlying much of the region is partially metamorphosed lava.

Beyond Black Marble Mountain, the PCT comes around another point, then circles through Big Rock Valley, a lakeless but beautiful glacial cirque with outstanding vistas and vast green meadows. Big Rock Camp, named for a huge, detached boulder, offers excellent camping. The PCT meets the Box Camp Trail at the north end of Big Rock Valley. From there, it's 2½ miles on the PCT to Paradise Lake and four miles on the Box Camp Trail to the Box Camp Trailhead, both along beautiful, 7000 foot ridges with many open areas, marble outcroppings and long vistas.

To drive to the Box Camp trailhead, continue up Canyon Creek Road from the Indian Scotty bridge, towards the Paradise Lake trailhead, instead of turning off at the Lovers Camp junction. The route is well marked.

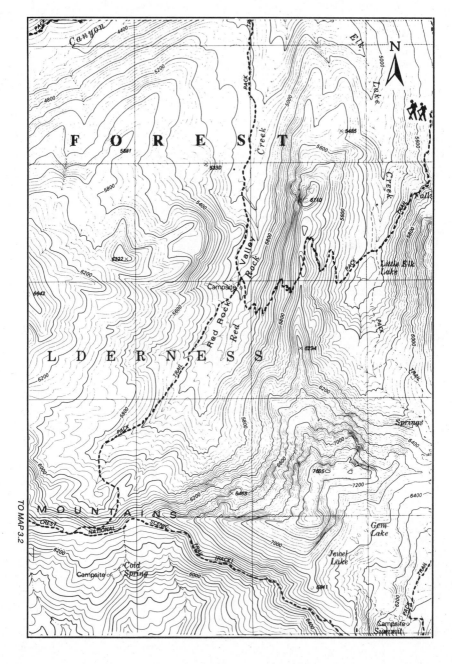

Map 3.1

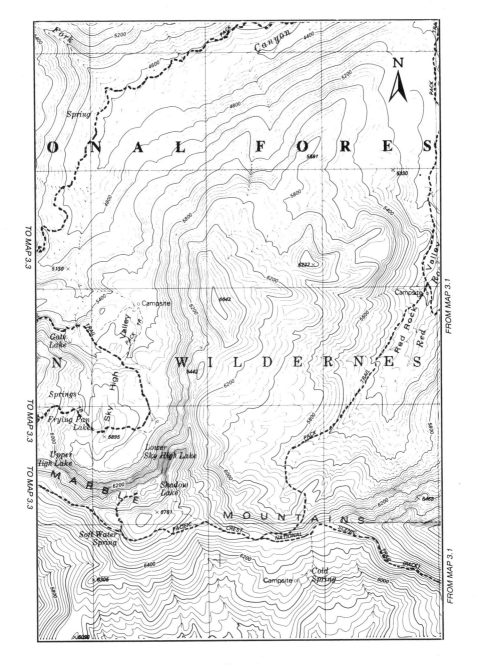

Map 3.2

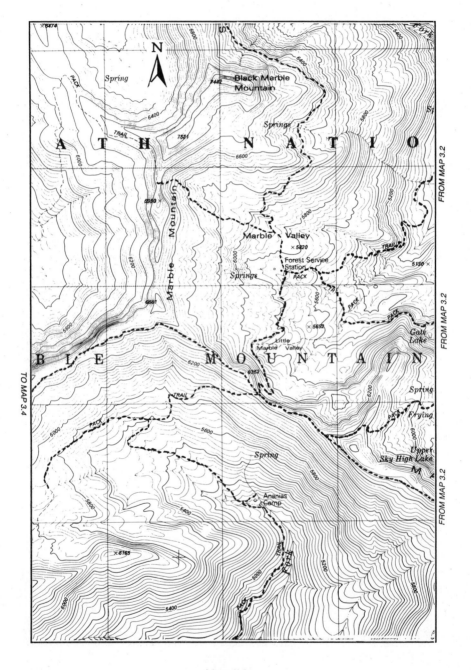

Map 3.3

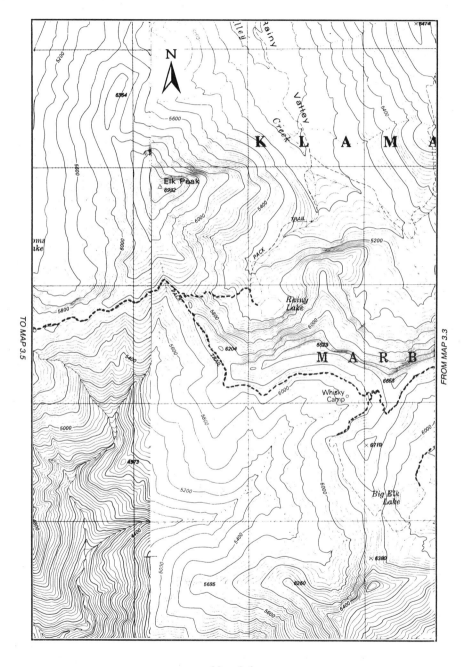

Map 3.4

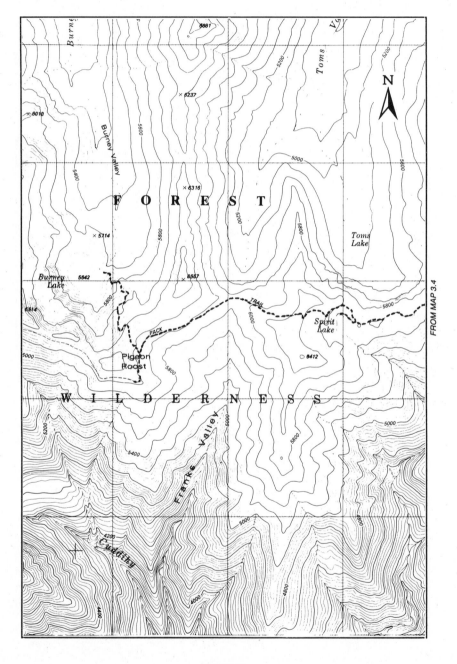

Map 3.5

4.   WRIGHT LAKES/DEEP LAKE

Destinations:	Boulder Creek Trail, Lower Wright Lake, Upper Wright Lake, Big Meadows, Second Valley, Deep Lake, Aspen Lake, Buckhorn Lake, Wolverine Lake, Chinquapin Lake.
Length:	4½ miles (Lower Wright Lake)
	5½ miles (Ridge above U. Wright)
	6 miles (Deep Lake)
Water:	Enough
Season:	June through October
Difficulty:	Extremely difficult
Elevation:	3800 to 7400 feet (Upper Wright)
	7700 feet (Ridge above U. Wright)
	6800 feet (Height of Deep Lake Trail)
	6350 feet (Deep Lake)
USGS 7.5" topo:	Boulder Peak
Location:	T44N-R11W-Sector 35
Use:	Non-motorized only
Use intensity:	Light
Camping:	Indian Scotty
Ownership:	Klamath National Forest
Phone:	(916) 468-5351

Directions: Take the south Yreka exit (Hwy 3) from I-5. Proceed to the town of Fort Jones and turn right, onto the Scott River Road. Go left over the Indian Scotty bridge, up Canyon Creek Road, and left again at the Boulder Creek Trail sign. This last spur, while steep and winding, is easily driveable. The trailhead is roomy and well marked, at a locked gate.

❖ ❖ ❖

Killer route #1: The Boulder Creek Trail

Some statistics: Boulder Peak, the black pyramid directly above Lower Wright Lake, is the Marble Mountains' highest summit at 8299 feet. Adjacent Upper Wright Lake ranks as the loftiest among the Wilderness Area's 90 lakes, at 7400 feet. Apart from these super-latives, the Wright Lakes/Boulder Peak area offers extreme beauty and some interesting botanical oddities.

If that isn't enough, a side trail, three miles from the trailhead, leads to Second Valley and the Deep Lake basin. No offense to the Wright Lakes, but Second Valley and Deep Lake may be the most exquisite, out of the way chunks of alpine splendor in the Marbles, aside from the Marble Valley and Maneaten lake.

There's a catch to all this. The preferred route to Wright and Deep Lakes is the Boulder Creek Trail, possibly the most demanding in the entire Wilderness. Many people attempt this path purely as a test of physical endurance. If you can handle Boulder Creek, you can handle anything.

The trail rises 2700 feet in its initial three miles, several long, level pitches and many outstanding vistas break up the drudgery. Should you survive to the Wright Lakes/Deep Lake junction, it's three more miles to Deep Lake, with an additional gain of 400 feet, then a loss of 500 feet. The Wright Lakes route rises 500 feet between the junc-tion and the lower lake (1½ miles), and another 700 feet in the final mile to the upper lake and high ridge.

While I hiked to Wright Lakes and Deep Lake on two separate day-hikes, five years apart, Boulder Creek is not a good day-hike can-didate because it is too tiring. My advice is to linger two or three days and see it all, taking in both Wright Lakes, Deep Lake, Second Valley, Little Elk Lake, the four lakes above Deep Lake and the top of Boul-der Peak.

At the Boulder Creek trailhead, the path begins in a middle eleva-tion Douglas-fir, ponderosa pine, sugar pine, white fir and incense cedar forest, mixed with black oak, madrone and canyon liveoak. The first mile shoots pretty much straight up, with a couple brief level stretches. This segment does not match most maps, which show the route following an old road over several long switchbacks. When the road became blocked by landslides, they rerouted the trail in a straight shot parallel to the creek, then along the top of an old clearcut.

After a mile, the path breaks out onto a closed road, which it follows for a much more moderate second mile. Grab your respite while you can. The third mile, back on the trail, is by far the worst, with two of the steepest extended upgrades I've ever experienced. This is an area that has been reworked by the Forest Service.

Between the two steepest pitches, the path breaks out into the open for ¼ mile and levels considerably. A panorama of Kings Castle, the Marble Rim and Black Marble Mountain comes into view here. The breathtaking scene remains visible over much of the Deep Lake route.

When the path emerges from the woods atop a narrow, rocky ridge, the worst is over. Soon after, back in the forest on a level flat, the trail divides. Continue straight for Second Valley and Deep Lake. Hang a left for Lower and Upper Wright Lakes.

The Wright Lakes: Truly sky high

A quarter-mile beyond the junction, in the Wright Lakes direction, the trail enters a beautiful meadowed basin with cliffs and waterfalls, wildflowers and towering peaks. Things continue rather steeply but nothing like before.

Lower Wright Lake occupies a vast, open glacial cirque, two cirques above the one near the junction. The starkness of the terrain make the lake appear much smaller than its 26 acres. The aqua pool, at 6900 feet, nestles against a black headwall which soars 1400 nearly vertical feet to Boulder Peak. Brook and rainbow trout fill the 90 foot deep lake.

Picturesque clumps of whitebark and foxtail pines decorate the immense meadow surrounding the lake on two sides. The former is a gnarled, treeline species which shows up infrequently in the Klamath mountains. Foxtail pine is also a treeline species, native mainly to the east side of the southern high Sierra. After a gap of 600 miles in its range, it turns up in widely scattered sites in the Marbles, Trinity Alps and Trinity Divide.

Wildflowers include a profusion of red and purple Indian paintbrush, arnica, aster, monkshood, fireweed, corn lily, monkey flower, pentstemon, delphinium, sedum, gentian and many others. Many occupy a seep area on the trail above the lower lake.

The 6½ acre Upper Wright Lake isn't as spectacular as its neighbor. Its basin is smaller and more confined, with a steeper, densely wooded (mountain hemlock and red fir) shore. The lake's is 50 feet deep and stocked with brook trout. At 7400 feet, Upper Wright Lake is the highest in the Marble Mountains.

The ultimate payoff comes ¼ mile beyond the upper lake, at the 7700 foot high ridge. There, the world falls away and a panorama of Scott Valley unfolds, with its patchwork ranchlands. In the distance, Mount Shasta pokes up its inevitable glaciated head. The other actively glaciated peak, far to the south, is Mount Thompson, highest in the Trinity Alps.

A trail to the right, from the ridgetop, skirts Boulder Peak, then drops into Second Valley. The Second Valley Trail meets the Deep Lake Trail three miles from the ridgetop and one mile from the Deep Lake/Wright Lakes junction. The ridgetop is the best place from which to climb Boulder Peak. The main trail, past the saddle above Upper Wright Lake, ends up at the Big Meadows trailhead in two miles.

Big Meadows, the elusive back door

On the map, the Big Meadows Trail appears to offer much easier access to the Wright Lakes than the Boulder Creek Trail. With a trailhead elevation of 6500 feet, by far the highest in the Marbles, it is three miles shorter and starts 2700 feet higher than the Boulder Creek, but still climbs 1200 feet in 2 miles.

Because the Big Meadows trailhead can be difficult to find and is on private property, it is not recommended. The road is long, steep and winding, with several treacherous spots. Since the entire road lies on private property, not a single sign navigates you through the maze and the trailhead is unmarked. It's a gorgeous trail, though, and Big

Meadows is worth a visit even if you don't make it to Upper Wright Lake. The trailhead itself, at the lower end of Big Meadows with a fantastic view of Scott Valley, offers an excellent destination. Expect snow at the trailhead well into June and rutted, muddy patches on the road well into July.

Here's how to get there: From Quartz Valley Road, out of Greenview in Scott Valley, turn onto the well marked gravel road (43N21) to the Shackleford Creek trailhead (Chapter 5). Four miles up Shackleford Creek Road, a sign points left and downhill for the Shackleford Trailhead. Take the uphill, right-hand road. After ½ mile, this steep but wide and well maintained link emerges onto another road. Head left here (which is actually straight ahead). Continue until you come to a turnoff marked by an orange painted rock pile. Turn right here. Soon after, the road levels and Big Meadows comes into view. After a mile, you'll see a spur road left, marked by a huge boulder with the word "Big" spray painted on it. Turn here, then bear left at the first intersection. This last road is steep and quite rough in spots but you'll make it with good tires and a little clearance.

Don't panic when you pass a side road heading uphill in the opposite direction with not enough room to turn (a small car can make it easily). If you continue straight for a few hundred feet, the road makes a loop which heads you in the right direction to get up the spur. Proceed to a logging landing at the top of the hill, where the trail begins. There's a wonderful campsite ⅛ mile down the road from the trailhead. Park at the edge of Big Meadows and walk across to the aspen grove. It's resplendent in autumn.

If you have complaints about the roads, lack of signs or logging activity, keep them to yourself. The owners are to be commended for permitting the public to drive their roads and to park at their trailhead. They could bar such use at any time.

(Note: The original directions given me for Big Meadows involved turning off Shackleford Creek Road 2½ miles sooner, at the wooden bridge over Snicktaw Creek. In September, 1995, I found the bridge washed out. A go-around through the creek looked too treacherous for my low clearance vehicle. Two weeks later, I returned with a friend who owned a Jeep Wrangler. We made it across the creek, over a large mound and all the way to Big Meadows. On the way back, we bottomed out on the mound, learning the painful lesson that it doesn't matter how many drive wheels you have if all are dangling in mid-air. A passing hunter pulled us out.)

At least two other routes lead to Big Meadows, including Big Meadows Road, a mile down Quartz Valley Road from the Shackleford turnoff. All are extremely complicated, rough and unsigned. The one I've described is by far the best.

From the trailhead, the path takes a briefly level route across Big Meadows to the Wilderness boundary and the Red Mountain Trail junction, both less than ¼ mile away. The Forest Service has tried valiantly to improve this first part of the trail through the meadows and bogs. The Red Mountain/Big Meadows junction sign was down when I visited and we were fortunate to notice the signless, 4x4 post lying in the grass. For the less observant, the main trail, which is the Red Mountain Trail, heads into a large draw with aspen trees and a creek, immediately beyond the Junction.

The Red Mountain Trail, which you don't take, contours across the steep, sparsely vegetated slope towards Red Mountain, an outcropping of weathered serpentinite just south of Boulder Peak and almost as high. This is a major foxtail pine area. Beyond Back Meadows (some maps say "Black Meadows"), the path drops down to Log Lake, on the Shackleford Creek Trail (Chapter 5), passing the turnoff to Calf and Long High Lakes on the way. Be aware that the Red Mountain Trail has been rerouted at Back Meadows Creek, crossing to the south side early on, and does not match the Wilderness map.

Turn right at the Red Mountain Trail junction for Wright Lakes, Boulder Peak and the rest of Big Meadows. The path scrambles steeply through grass, floral meadows, aspen groves and occasional forested pockets to the saddle above Upper Wright Lake. Views of Scott Valley, Mount Shasta, the Trinity Alps and the Marbles improve with each step, with the Shackleford and Kidder Creek areas especially prominent

The path left from the saddle between Big Meadows and Upper Wright Lake, leads to Second Valley and Deep Lake. (Note: the Wright Lake/Second Valley junction is at the saddle, which is not quite how the map shows it). To climb Boulder Peak, follow this route for ¼ mile until you see another saddle a few hundred feet up the hill, beside the main rise of Boulder Peak. Scramble up to the saddle (above Lower Wright Lake), then climb the bouldery ridge to the summit. It should take 30 to 45 minutes.

Deep Lake: Not so deep but magnificent

The Wright Lakes would not be my first choice as a destination from the Boulder Creek Trail. As gorgeous as they are, Deep Lake is prettier. And Second Valley offers the ultimate closeup of Boulder Peak.

From the Wright Lakes/Deep Lake junction, the Deep Lake Trail zooms uphill, rising 300 feet in ¼ mile. After coming around a precarious rocky crest (high point of the Deep Lake route at 6800 feet), it enters the huge Second Valley Creek drainage, clinging to a rocky, treeless, nearly vertical hillside 2500 feet above Canyon Creek. Look for parked cars at Lovers Camp, far, far below.

This precarious trail segment slowly makes its way around to the creek, which plunges down the mountainside in a series of cascades and waterfalls. After a while, the black tower of Boulder peak comes into view on the left.

Second Valley proper, a mile from the junction, is a total surprise which is not visible until you're actually in it. It's what they call a "hanging valley," a flat bottomed basin whose mouth and creek drop abruptly over a table-edge rim as they plunge into the much larger and steeper Canyon Creek Valley.

Stunning Second Valley offers the ultimate view of Boulder Peak, which forms its east wall. Equally imposing black schist cliffs make up the basin's headwall and west flank. In-between, brilliant green meadows are cut by a meandering creek and small ponds. In my June visit, patches of snow dotted the crags and upper meadows. It's a superb, centrally located camping spot.

The junction of the Second Valley and Deep Lake Trails is unsigned. Immediately upon hitting the creek and entering Second Valley, look for a faint path heading west, away from Second Valley, beginning just across the creek at the valley mouth. Follow this for

Deep Lake. For Upper Wright Lake, Boulder Peak and Big Meadows, take the trail up Second Valley.

Beyond the Second Valley turnoff, the Deep Lake Trail works its way around a second point, then through an old burn from the 1987 fires. It then enters the steep Muse Meadow drainage, dropping sharply at first but levelling off. The mouth of the Deep Lake basin can be seen at the drainage's far end, on the left.

A mile later, coming around a point and over a small, rocky crest, the path enters the Deep Lake basin, a large glacial cirque ringed in bare outcroppings and carpeted with a giant, rolling, emerald meadow, much like Lower Wright Lake. Immediately after, the turn-off to Elk Lake is passed.

It's a fair distance, mostly uphill, across the meadow to Deep Lake, tucked against the base of the headwall. Artistically placed clusters of whitebark pine, Western white pine and mountain mahogany tie the various elements together.

The brilliant aqua lake covers 16 acres and reaches a depth of 68 feet. Despite the name, Ukonom, Cliff, Maneaten and Lower Wright Lakes are deeper than Deep Lake. None are prettier, however. Deep Lake houses a population of brook, rainbow and brown trout.

An alternate route to Deep Lake begins at the popular Lovers Camp trailhead (Chapter 3). At 4200 feet, Lovers Camp is 400 feet higher than the Boulder Creek trailhead. It's seven miles from Lovers Camp to Deep Lake, versus six via Boulder Creek. From a turnoff 2 ½ miles up the Red Rock Valley Trail out of Lovers Camp, the path climbs up and down a steep ridge to Little Elk Lake, then makes a three mile contour around to Deep Lake. While I far prefer the Boulder Creek route, more than half of Deep Lake visitors begin at Lover's Camp.

Little Elk Lake lies three miles from, and 900 feet below, Deep Lake (5400 feet versus 6300 feet), in yet another exquisite glacial basin. The six acre pool, while only five feet deep, houses a naturally reproducing population of rainbow and brown trout. Oddly, Little Elk Lake is larger than Big Elk Lake, seven miles away on the other side of Marble Valley.

To complete your Deep Lake/Wright Lakes excursion, hike up the head of the Deep Lake basin, to the ledge immediately above (and

700 feet higher). While there's no trail, the route is obvious. It's the only way up the Deep Lake headwall not involving vertical rock faces. The ledge houses four small, extremely lovely, rock lined lakes: Aspen (5½ acres, 58 feet deep, brook trout), Buckhorn (2 acres, 25 feet deep, eastern brook and rainbow trout), Wolverine (1½ acres, 11 feet deep, a few brookies), and Chinquapin (3½ acres, 25 feet deep, brook and rainbow trout).

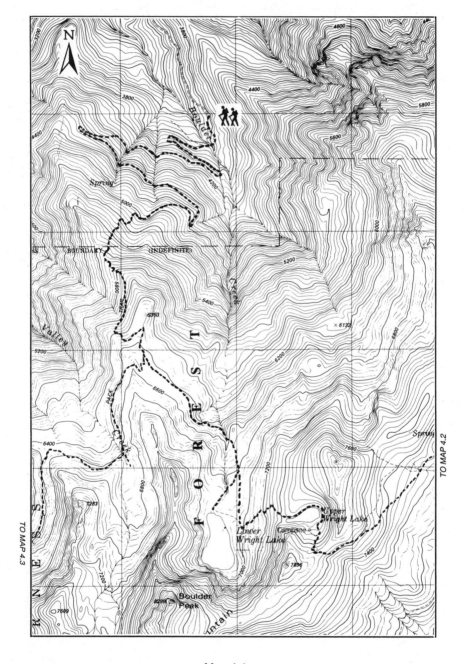

Map 4.1

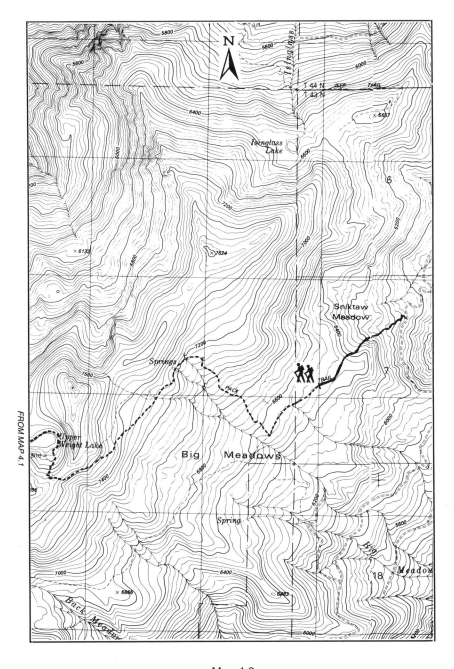

Map 4.2

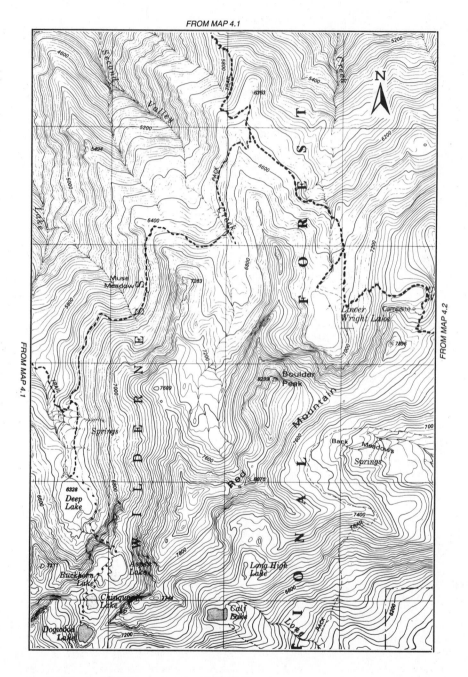

Map 4.3

5.

SHACKLEFORD CREEK/CLIFF, CAMPBELL, SUMMIT LAKES

Destinations:	Shackleford Creek, Log Lake, Log Lake Meadow, Calf Lake, Summit Lake, Summit Meadow Lake, Campbell Lake, Cliff Lake.
Length:	3½ miles (Log Lake),
	4½ miles (Campbell Lake)
	5 miles (Cliff Lake)
	5½ miles (Summit Lake)
	13 mile loop, all lakes
Difficulty:	Moderate
Elevation:	4400 to 5400 feet (Log Lake)
	5800 feet (Campbell Lake)
	6100 feet (Cliff Lake)
	6000 feet (Summit Lake)
Season:	May through November (Log Lake)
	June through October (other lakes)
Location:	T43N-R10W-Sector 19
Water:	Everywhere
USGA 7.5" topo:	Boulder Peak
Ownership:	Klamath National Forest
Phone:	916) 468-5351
Camping:	At trailhead
Use:	Non-motorized only
Use intensity:	Heavy

Directions: Take I-5 to the south Yreka/Scott Valley exit. From there, follow Highway-3 past Fort Jones to Greenview. Turn right at Greenview, onto Quartz Valley Road and continue to the well marked Shackleford Creek turnoff, bearing left when in doubt. It's seven miles, up a wide, dirt and gravel road, to the roomy trailhead, with pit toilets, alongside Shackleford Creek.

Shackleford Creek and Log Lake: A path for all seasons

This second most popular route in the Marbles (after Lovers Camp/Canyon Creek), visiting some of the Wilderness Area's largest and most splendid lakes, is easy for the first three miles and scenic throughout. Even the access road and trailhead are scenic, following a steep walled canyon to a picturesque campsite along a rushing creek. Log Lake, at 5400 feet, makes an accessible early season destination while Cliff Lake ranks as the Marbles' second largest, after Ukonom Lake (Chapter 9).

The path hugs Shackleford Creek for five miles to Summit Lake. The initial ½ mile, along an old road bed to the Wilderness boundary, rises slightly. After that, things level off until the junction below Log Lake.

Even if you only hike to this first junction, it's worth it. Shackleford Creek is wide, fast and scenic as it courses through the canyon. The trail, crossing numerous small side creeks, makes its way through a chain of green, corn lily meadows. In my April visit, I found patches of snow near the trailhead and vast snowfields blanketing the higher meadows. Somehow, the trail missed nearly all of them until just past Log Lake, where I was finally forced to turn back.

The junction below Log Lake lies three miles up the path. The arrow left says "Campbell Lake - 1 mile" while the one pointing right announces, "Campbell Lake - 1½ miles." With an elevation gain of 800 feet between this lower junction and Campbell Lake, I'd advise the longer route, saving the shorter one for the trip home. The long route is much prettier, visiting Log Lake and Log Lake Meadows and offering the best access to Summit and Cliff Lakes.

In my April visit, the shorter route required fording Shackleford Creek, which looked knee deep and treacherous. By June, the creek had calmed down. A fallen tree, spanning the creek several hundred feet upstream, appeared unsafe.

Approaching Log Lake, the path rises 400 feet in ½ mile in a series of switchbacks. Log Lake itself is minuscule, only an acre, although

I'm told brook trout fishing is pretty good in the green, log strewn water.

Just before Log Lake, the primitive Calf Lake Trail takes off to the right. It's a rugged two miles, rising 500 feet the first mile and 1100 feet the second, to Calf Lake, a three acre, 30 foot deep puddle in a red rock pocket at 7100 feet. The Lake is stocked with brook trout. From Calf Lake, it's an easy, ¼ mile shot to the northeast to Long High Lake, a 1½ acre, six foot deep pool at 7150 feet, stocked with brook trout. By contouring west ½ mile from Calf Lake, through a wide gap, you'll end up at Dogwood Lake, part of the chain of four small lakes in the rock ledge basin above Deep Lake (Chapter 4).

Above Calf Lake, four additional uphill miles on the Red Mountain Trail takes you to the Big Meadows Trail, which leads to Upper Wright Lake and the Big Meadows trailhead (Chapter 4).

South and west of Log Lake, a picturesque semi-circle of black crags rises 2000 feet above the woods. In April, 10 feet of snow filled its crevices and lower slopes. North of Log Lake, a brushy mountainside soars hundreds of feet upward, with a creek plunging down in a series of waterfalls.

At Log Lake in my April visit, I talked to a fellow who had made it to Campbell Lake. He said the snow there was four feet deep and continuous. I admired his determination and was amazed to encounter so many hikers so early in the season.

Shortly beyond Log Lake, the path rejoins Shackleford Creek, which runs through the middle of Log Lake Meadow, an extensive splotch of marshy greenery resplendent with wildflowers.

Towards the end of the meadow, ¼ mile past Log Lake, a side trail takes off left, to Campbell and Cliff Lakes. It's a mile up the side trail to Campbell Lake and 1½ miles to Cliff Lake.

Where the Cliff/Campbell cut-off crosses Log Lake Meadow, Shackleford Creek braids into several channels. Thus, there are three creek crossings here instead of one. While none are very deep, there are no large rocks to step on so count on getting your shoes wet. Beyond Log Lake Meadow, the cut-off trail gains 400 feet as it winds through the woods and onto the Campbell Lake bench.

Summit Lake, or summit-thing like that

For Summit Lake, continue straight instead of turning left at the junction above Log Lake. It's two miles, along a moderately rising tread, to Summit Lake and Summit Meadow Lake.

Shackleford Creek continues to entertain in this segment, with meadows, benches and low waterfalls highlighting the mostly open route. Note the high cliff on the opposite side of the valley. Should you return via Campbell Lake, you'll pass over the top of it. Note also the Little Elk Lake primitive trail, $\frac{1}{2}$ mile before Summit Lake. It's $2\frac{1}{2}$ extremely difficult miles, over a rocky, 6800 foot gap, to Little Elk Lake. Little Elk Lake is much more easily (although not easily) reached from Lovers Camp (Chapter 3) or the Boulder Creek Trail (Chapter 4).

Just before Summit Lake, a $\frac{3}{4}$ mile spur rising 400 feet, connects to the Pacific Crest Trail, on its way from the Sky High area to Maneaten Lake. The quickest route to Maneaten Lake, which has no trail access, is via Kidder Lake (Chapter 6).

Summit Lake is the source of Shackleford Creek. Covering five acres at the base of a low, black headwall, the 6000 foot pool reaches a depth of 15 feet and is stocked with brook trout. The encircling woods contains many fine campsites.

In my June visit, I found patches of snow and several extremely muddy stretches at Summit Lake. I also encountered much fog, got snowed on, became lost on a false trail and saw almost none of the lake. Had I not brought a flannel shirt (it's my rule always to bring a jacket no matter how nice the weather), the excursion could have ended in disaster. It was warm and sunny at the trailhead.

The meadow containing Summit Meadow Lake begins immediately above Summit Lake. The elongated lake, at the base of a low dirt headwall, covers $1\frac{1}{2}$ acres, is four feet deep and houses a few brook trout.

Beyond the Summit Lake area, the path gradually doubles back on itself as it works its way around the head of the Shackleford Creek valley. Immediately after Summit Meadow Lake, it climbs through the woods and over a ridge, then loses 500 feet in $\frac{1}{2}$ mile. The 6300 foot ridgetop is the route's highest elevation.

After a series of ponds and small meadows, the path arrives at yet another junction. Turn right for Cliff Lake and left for Campbell Lake, Log Lake and the trailhead.

Cliff and Campbell Lakes: The big and the beautiful

Cliff Lake lies at the end of a winding spur which rises 400 feet in ½ mile, up a series of rocky ledges. There's a great view of Campbell Lake early on. One of the Marbles' most impressive and popular bodies of water, Cliff Lake occupies a deep cirque whose precipitous headwall rises 1300 feet from the water and often retains snow well into July.

At 52 acres, Cliff Lake is second in the Marbles to Ukonom Lake. With a depth of 175 feet, it is by far the deepest in the Wilderness (and nearly three times as deep as Deep Lake). Rainbow, brook and brown trout lurk in its blue waters. The open forest stands on its rocky shore contain numerous (too many in the view of some), excellent campsites.

While Campbell Lake, perched on a densely forested bench rather than tucked inside a glacial cirque, isn't quite up to Cliff Lake's scenic standards, it is the Marbles' fourth largest at 33 acres, with a depth of 30 feet. Fishing from its sinuous, occasionally rocky shore, is supposed to be excellent, with rainbow, brook and brown trout awaiting lucky anglers.

There are two routes back from Campbell Lake. The high end of the Log Lake cut-off comes in just past Campbell Lake, shortly beyond where the path re-enters the woods. The turnoff is easily missed so look for a sign on the left. For the shortcut to the junction below Log Lake, continue straight, around Campbell's north shore, to a trail along the outlet creek.

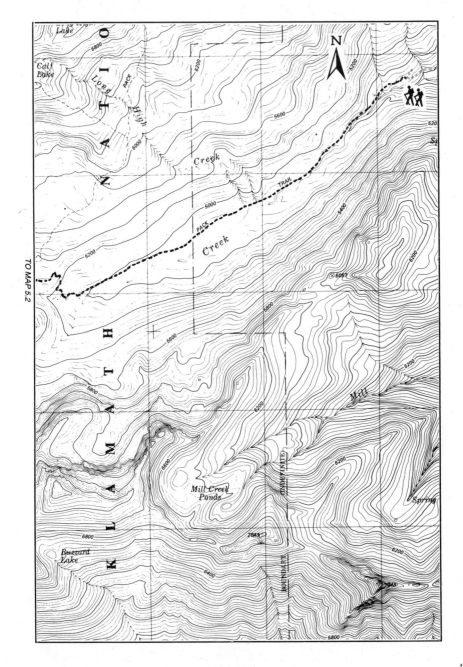

Map 5.1

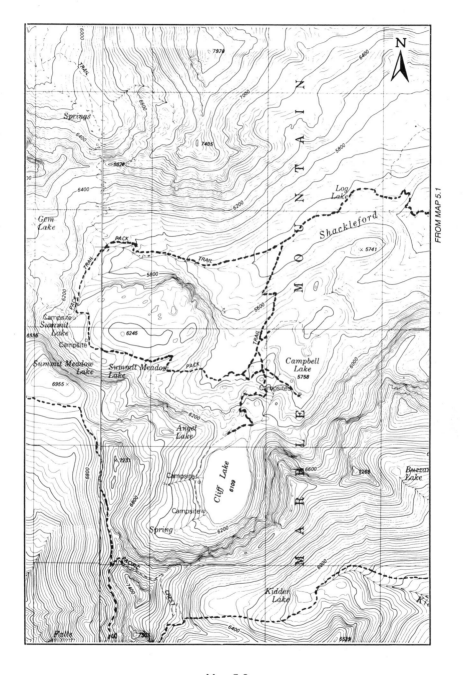

Map 5.2

6.
KIDDER LAKE/MANEATEN LAKE/SHELLY FORK

Destinations:	Kidder Lake, Maneaten Lake, Fisher Lake, Marten Lake, Kleaver Lake, Milne Lake, Wooley Lake, Blueberry Lake, Shelly Lake, Pacific Crest Trail.
Length	3½ miles (Kidder Lake)
	3½ miles (Shelly Lake)
	5 miles (Maneaten Lake)
Difficulty:	Moderate
Elevation:	4800 to 5900 feet (Kidder)
	6700 feet (Shelly Lake)
	6200 feet (Maneaten Lake)
	7000 feet (Notch above Maneaten Lake)
	6700 feet (Wooley Lake)
Season:	May through November (Kidder)
	June through October (others)
Water:	Lots
USGS 7.5" topo:	Boulder Peak, Marble Mountain
Location:	T43N-R10W-Sector 7
Use intensity:	Moderate
Ownership:	Siskiyou National Forest
Phone:	(916) 468-5351

Directions: From I-5, take the south Yreka exit and follow Highway-3 to Greenview. At Greenview, turn right onto Quartz Valley Road, left two blocks later on Main Street and right after two more blocks onto Kidder Creek Road. Proceed past the pavement end, several miles into the canyon, to a wooden bridge over Kidder Creek. Just before the bridge, bear right, on the uphill fork. This 1½ mile segment contains areas of loose gravel where your tires may spin a little. Proceed to a sharp uphill switchback. Continue straight at the switchback, on a slightly downward spur. There are no road numbers or signs.

The trailhead is located several hundred yards up the final spur, with room for a dozen cars. The gravel access roads are a little bumpy and narrow but driveable, except for a greater than average accumulation of loose rocks fallen from the cutbanks.

Kidder Lake. No kidding

With no signs and an access road beginning in downtown Greenview, beautiful Kidder Lake has remained the domain of Scott Valley residents. I know about it only because I happen to be a former Scott Valleyite. Even if you never reach the lake, this is an attractive, well hidden, easily accessed area. Just before a wooden auto bridge, seven or eight miles out of Greenview, Kidder Creek squeezes through an impressive, narrow rock gorge.

The only problem with all this beauty is that it is private property, including the trailhead and all access roads. Over the wooden auto bridge spanning Kidder Creek, a maze of private roads enables you to drive to exquisite glacial basins on the Babs, Glendenning and Shelly Forks. Bear in mind that public use is at the discretion of the owner. Because the roomy trailhead lies on private property, trailhead markers are inside the Wilderness boundary, several hundred yards down the path.

From the Kidder Creek trailhead, it's 3½ miles to Kidder Lake and 5 to Maneaten Lake. The Forest Service has finally taken down a misleading sign claiming it was five miles to Kidder Lake.

The trail's initial mile is fairly level as it makes its way through an inspiring old growth woods of Douglas-fir and sugar pine, high above and out of sight of the creek. Look for a small burn area and a couple of impressive side creeks. After a mile, the path drops to the water's edge at a level flat near a deep and clear pool—a great fishing and swimming spot. At 4600 feet elevation, it's an excellent campsite or short day-hike destination. Look for ½ dozen quaking aspens in the vicinity. Aspen, infrequent but not rare in the Marbles, usually shows up at much higher elevations. In my May visit, a field of serviceberry bushes around the aspens were resplendent in white, cherry-looking blossoms. Cherry and serviceberry both belong to the Rose family.

The second mile follows the creek to the Hayes Meadow Trail turnoff, named for a founder of Greenview. The town used to be called Hayes Corners. The forest association of Douglas-fir, sugar pine, white fir and ponderosa pine, continues almost to Kidder Lake, where Shasta red fir and mountain hemlock suddenly take over. Look for vanillaleaf, princess pine, dwarf Oregongrape and hazelnut in the forest understory and an area of huge trees, blown over by wind, just before the Hayes Meadow junction.

Beyond the junction, the heretofore level path steepens markedly, rising 1100 feet in 1½ miles. A highlight is a 75 foot waterfall hidden in the woods ½ mile before the lake. A short side path offers a fine closeup view. The waterfall tumbles over a vertical cliff, which the trail then climbs. After ascending a moist draw choked with mountain alder and mud, the path winds out onto bare rock briefly, with a panorama of the canyon below, framing Mount Shasta in the distance. If you're heading for Maneaten Lake, you should know that this vista, impressive as it is, offers only the meagerest hint of vistas to come.

Shallow and green, Kidder Lake covers only two acres and is stocked with rainbow trout. The shoreline is varied, with meadow in some spots, woods in others and brush in others. The postcard scene is dominated by a low headwall at the far end, with a massive, double-pointed rock crag rising above.

Maneaten Lake. Yum!!

Maneaten Lake may be the most beautiful in the Marble Mountains, a Wilderness famous for its many splendid alpine lakes. Maneaten is a miniature version of Sapphire Lake, which is my nominee (along with Grizzly Lake), for the most beautiful in the adjacent and much larger Trinity Alps Wilderness. However, reaching Maneaten's deeply gouged cirque basin requires a major effort. The task was recently made somewhat easier by the "re-routing" of the Pacific Crest Trail. Maneaten Lake is popular among Scott Valleyites, despite monstrous access problems which, supposedly, have eaten a few men.

Above Kidder Lake, the Kidder Creek Trail continues for a mile, rising 700 feet on its way to a rendezvous with the PCT. The latter runs just below the rugged, glacially sculpted eastern crest of the Wilderness Area's main east-west divide. The Forest Service map shows the upper Kidder Creek Trail incorrectly. It has it charging up the middle of the wide, grassy basin above Kidder Lake, climbing with horriffic steepness the last ¼ mile to the PCT. In real life, the path makes a couple of switchbacks up the wooded slope just south of the lake, then emerges atop the ridge between Kidder and Hayes Creeks. After that, it follows the ridge moderately uphill to the PCT.

The place where the Kidder Creek Trail hits the Kidder-Hayes Ridge, may be the most suddenly surprising and awe inspiring places anywhere. Keeping in mind that the scenery has been outstanding all along, the path breaks out of the woods and a line of dramatic, snow capped, rocky peaks pops into view, decorated with high meadows, profuse wildflowers, immense glacial basins and miles of glacially polished rock. Far below, to the south, lies Hayes Meadow, whose access trail was passed a mile below Kidder Lake. The lakeless Hayes Meadow basin is much larger and more impressive than the Kidder Lake basin, which is pretty spectacular in its own right. Theoretically, the Hayes Meadow Trail ties back into the Kidder Creek Trail at the ridgetop. It didn't see it.

As you hike up the ridgetop, look for a high gap on the northwest horizon. Cliff Lake (Chapter 5), second largest in the Wilderness, lies just on the other side. Southeast from the ridgetop, you'll see a narrow, "V" shaped notch, with a few trees, large snowfields and a rock bench just below. Maneaten Lake lies just over the notch. Behind you, and dominating everything, lies the deep canyon of Kidder Creek, still framing Mount Shasta.

No sign marked the Kidder Creek/PCT Junction, which could confuse PCT travelers. For Maneaten Lake, head south on the PCT from the junction, descending slightly for ½ mile, to a meadow just below the notch. This is a gorgeous spot, with a small pond on a rock shelf, an impressive waterfall and snowfields lingering far into summer. On my August 8th visit, I had to traverse two large snow fields to reach the notch.

Just before the PCT crosses the creek flowing down from the notch, another junction turns up, between the PCT and a route called the "PCT Alternate." The sign is unobtrusive and little is made of this junction. Northbound PCT travelers should know that the Alternate was constructed not to access Maneaten Lake but to bypass an often impassible PCT section north of Kidder Lake. The trail is an Alternate because only Congress can reroute the PCT.

The PCT must be pretty bad if the Alternate is the preferred route. From the junction, the Alternate ascends 300 magnificent feet in 1/4 mile, in a series of switchbacks through a small stand of mountain hemlock and white pine, to an elevation of 7000 feet at the notch. From the notch, Maneaten Lake appears, 800 feet straight down. The Alternate descends 200 of the 800 feet, in rapid switchbacks, before trailing off north, towards Cliff Lake and away from Maneaten Lake. While the off-trail scramble from the Alternate to the lake wasn't as difficult as I'd heard, the hike back up was predictably gruelling.

Covering 14 acres in a barren, austere, schist and serpentine cirque which could have been carved with a ice cream scoop, Maneaten Lake is the epitome of a high mountain glacial lake. The clear, emerald water reaches a depth of 112 feet and produces large rainbow trout. Surrounded by cliffs up to 1500 feet high, rock outcroppings and scree slopes form the shoreline. In my August visit, snowbanks 10 feet deep lined the banks on the south side. The northern shore is more accessible, formed by a rock bench rising only 30 or 40 feet above the water. I did notice one level patch at the water's edge, with even a couple of trees, on the northeast shore. The lake's outlet flows into a magnificent waterfall which, depending on the time of year, either dribbles or crashes 800 feet into the Wooley Creek valley. Maneaten Lake is the source of Wooley Creek, the Wilderness Area's principal drainage.

If you continue south on the PCT instead of taking the Alternate to Maneaten Lake, you'll come to Marten and Fisher Lakes after 1 1/2 miles. From the ridgetop on the Kidder Lake Trail, if you visually scan the semi-circular rim of the giant Hayes Meadow cirque as it trails southward, you'll observe a little rock bench, far in the distance, just below the rim's lip. Marten and Fisher Lakes occupy this bench. Both lie alongside the PCT and boast fine campsites. The shallow, grassy shored lakes cover an acre each, at 6200 feet elevation, and contain brook and rainbow trout. The lakes were named for a comedy team popular in the 1950's. After Jerry left, Dean replaced him with Eddie.

Actually, the lakes are named for nocturnal, weasel-like animals which inhabit the area but which you're never likely to encounter.

Wooley Lake and furry water

Wooley Lake is a far more difficult trek than Maneaten Lake but nearly as spectacular. Either: (1) Contour south two miles, from the PCT above Maneaten Lake, out of the cirque and past Milne Lake and the tiny Heather Lake ponds. This route is much shorter than Option #2 but involves much perpendicular ground. Since it is also barren ground with long vistas, it is fairly easy to remain oriented on an off-trail hike. (2) Take the Bug Gulch Trail from the PCT junction at Shelly Meadows. Six miles from the junction (8½ miles from the Shelly Fork trailhead), at Grants Meadow, proceed to the upper end of the meadow and climb out of the basin to the left of the main peak (a one mile trek climbing 1100 feet). You should end up on the rim above Wooley Lake, 600 feet above the water.

Wooley Lake covers 6½ acres at 6700 feet, in a barren, steep-walled, metavolcanic basin similar to Maneaten Lake. It is extremely deep at 84 feet. The shore is exposed and rocky and, as with Maneaten Lake, the outlet creek forms an impressive waterfall over a rock ledge. Though seldom visited, it is stocked with rainbow trout. Blueberry Lake lies ½ mile below Wooley Lake, down the outlet creek which also happens to be the South Fork of Wooley Creek (Chapter 8). It covers 1½ acres, is 10 feet deep and contains brook trout.

Should you make it to Wooley Lake, head northwest through the large meadow on the lake's north side, then contour left (west), along the base of, then around, the ridge. With luck, you'll end up at

Kleaver Lake, which covers 2½ acres at 6500 feet. It is 17 feet deep and stocked with brook trout. Milne Lake sits ¼ mile above Kleaver Lake and a couple hundred feet uphill. It also covers 2½ acres, with a depth of 39 feet and an elevation of 6750 feet. Brook and rainbow trout can be had. Both lakes occupy extremely rocky pockets and have bouldery, open shores.

Shelly Fork and Keats spoon

To reach the Shelly Fork Trail, cross the bridge over Kidder Creek, just before the Kidder Creek trailhead. Continue uphill, briefly, to a three way intersection and take the right hand fork. While the road is a little rough and steep at first, its worst problem is a couple of very deep waterbars, which could turn back a small car. It is 1 ½ miles, through Shelly Fork Creek and around a tight switchback, to the un-marked trailhead at a logging landing.

The difficult path climbs 2000 feet in 2½ miles, tightly hugging the creek and crossing it a couple times, as it makes its way to the head of the basin, an impressive glacial cirque ringed by a rocky headwall. The first mile traverses a dense woods. After that, the path gets into much more open terrain.

The PCT comes in at the ridgetop saddle. If you continue on the Shelly Fork Trail instead of turning onto the PCT, you'll gradually circle down into Bug Gulch, then head up over Bear Wallow Peak, then drop down into Grants Gulch. These are all fine places, espe-cially Bug Gulch. Should you opt to head south (left) on the PCT, at the Shelly Fork divide, it's ½ mile to Wilson Cabin and Shelly Mead-ows, both superb camping spots. Another ½ mile on the PCT takes you to the Shelly Lake outlet. Shelly Lake lies ¼ mile away, at the end of a rugged hike up the access creek, on a rocky bench at the foot of a 7200 foot peak. It covers 5½ acres at 6700 feet, is 43 feet deep and is stocked with brook and rainbow trout.

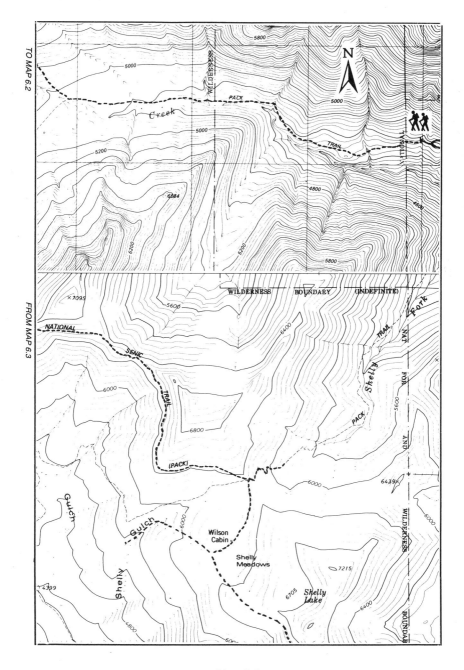

Map 6.1

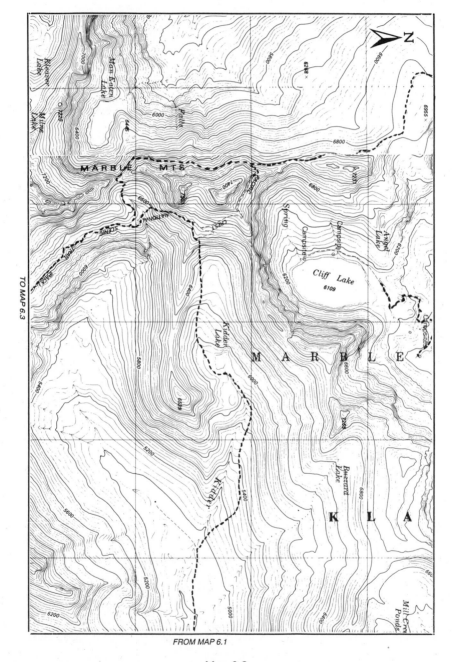

FROM MAP 6.1

Map 6.2

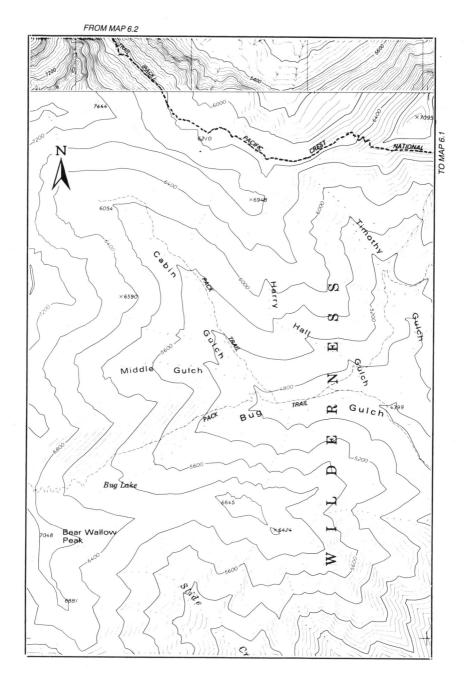

Map 6.3

7.

HANCOCK LAKE/NORTH FORK SALMON/LITTLE NORTH FORK

Destinations:	North Fork Salmon River, Lake of the Islands, Abbott Lake, Wild Lake, Ethel Lake, Katherine Lake, Horse Range Lakes, English Lake. Hancock Lake, English Peak, Pine Lake, Little North Fork, Clear Lake, Lost Lake, Chimney Rock, Chimney Rock Lake, Steinacher Lake.
Length:	13 miles to Hancock Lake, via No. Fork, Little No. Fork and Garden Gulch.
Water:	Usually adequate. Be careful on Garden Gulch Trail after mid-summer.
Season:	High Lakes - June through October. River trails - any.
Difficulty:	Moderate to difficult
Elevation:	2100 feet (Little North Fork trailhead)
	2900 feet (North Fork trailhead)
	4200 feet (Garden Gulch trailhead)
	7350 feet (English Peak)
	6400 feet (Hancock Lake)
USGS 7.5" topo:	Yellow Dog Peak, English Peak, Medicine Mountain, Sawyers Bar, Forks of Salmon
Location:	41N-R11W-Sec 35 (N. Fork)
	T40N-R12W-Sector 24 (Little N. Fork)
	T40N-R12W-Sector 14 (Garden Gulch)
Use intensity:	Light
Camping:	Idlewild CG
Phone:	1-916-467-5757

Directions: From I-5, take the south Yreka exit and follow Highway-3 to Etna. In Etna, turn right (west) on Main Street and take the mostly paved road over Etna Summit towards Sawyers Bar and the North Fork of the Salmon River. Three trailheads access the Hancock Lake/English Peak region off the Sawyers Bar Road.

North Fork Salmon. Turn right onto dirt road 41N37, at Idlewild Campground at the bottom of Etna Summit, and follow it to the trailhead, which accommodates a dozen cars with trailers. The trail begins at the footbridge.

Little North Fork. Beyond Sawyers Bar and just past the Little North Fork mouth, take the first right. Proceed uphill a mile to the well marked trailhead. There's parking for eight cars at a turnout along the shoulder.

Garden Gulch. Continue past the Little North Fork trailhead, around several switchbacks, to a steep side road on the right. The sign at the side road has fallen over but is barely readable. It's another mile to the trailhead, which is unmarked but obvious, with parking for six cars.

The North Fork Trail: A really long shortcut

Deep in the heart of the Marble Mountains, more remote even than Burney or Ukonom Lakes (Chapters 3 and 9), lies one of the most magnificent mountain complexes in the American wilderness system. The area's core, English Peak and Hancock Lake, is reached by lengthy trails from the Salmon River, itself one of California's most isolated treasures.

My disastrous attempt at exploring the Hancock Lake area via the Little North Fork and Garden Gulch Trails, shall be described shortly. Suffice to say, there's a reason the North Fork Trail is more popular than these other routes.

On the map, the North Fork Trail appears far longer than Little North Fork or Garden Gulch. Actually, it's 13 miles to Hancock Lake via all three entries. The Little North Fork's main drawbacks are: (1) The trail rarely meets the river. (2) A killer hill (The Snowslide Gulch Trail), rising 2200 feet in 2 miles.

The hill can be avoided by going via Hamilton Camp, which extends the trip by two miles and is still pretty steep. The Garden Gulch Trail begins much higher than the two river trails, at 4200 feet, but climbs 2400 feet in its first 2½ miles.

The North Fork Trail, while easier than the others and starting 800 feet higher than the Little North Fork, is not all peaches and gravy. Its worst pitch climbs 2000 feet in three miles. Face it, to visit Hancock Lake, you're going to have to walk a long way and climb a lot. Lots of folks do it.

The North Fork Trail begins in a low elevation woods by the river, which pretty much describes the first 11 miles. While it's a handsome river, with vast, wooded slopes, wide, level bars, occasional rock gorges and waterfalls, and great campsites everywhere you look, it's a long way before you get to anything. The path climbs to a couple hundred feet above the water every now and then, but all in all, it hugs the bank. Several picturesque side creeks are crossed, especially at Big Creek, Right Hand Fork and Lake of the Islands Creek.

The initial 11 miles, until the ascent into the high country, is prime salmon and steelhead habitat, including summer steelhead. The North Fork ranks among Northern California's finest fishing streams.

The low elevation woods are typical, Douglas-fir, ponderosa pine, sugar pine, incense cedar, madrone, black oak, tanoak and canyon liveoak. The last indicates thin soils and shaded slopes. Along the river, look for willow, cottonwood, red alder, bigleaf maple, vine maple and elephant ears. Abundant evergreen huckleberry and thimbleberry makes a fine late season treat. On the peaks and at the lakes, white pine, white fir, mountain hemlock, red fir and occasional lodgepole pine dominate.

From Mule Bridge at the trailhead, it's two miles to a couple of cabins in a cedar grove (in the distance below), then two more to Abbott Ranch. On the way, you pass some outstanding swimming holes, with a fine campsite and swimming hole at Big Creek. The bridge just before Abbott Ranch, over a narrow rock gorge, is the trail's last. At numerous crossings above Abbott Ranch, you risk being turned back any season other than mid-summer to late fall.

At mile 5½, the Right Hand Fork Trail comes in. After fording the North Fork, the Right Hand Fork route continues to Shelly Meadows, eight miles away (Chapter 6). Past the Right Hand Fork junction, the main trail, which has been trending northward, gradually swings west.

It is 1½ miles beyond the Right Hand Fork junction to yet another crossing, with another at mile eight, near the Lake of the Islands junction. Many of these crossings involve wading so be prepared to get your feet wet.

The first real highlight comes at mile 8½, at the Lake of the Island turnoff. To reach the lake, you have to (yes) cross the river. The elevation at the junction is 4200 feet while the lake sits two miles away, up a beautiful, if brushy, path with aspen groves at the high end. Lake of the Island is a 13 acre, 25 feet deep pool at 5600 feet, with brook and rainbow trout. The shore is sparsely wooded, with a dramatic headwall rising above the far end, a small island in the middle and outstanding campsites. The lake's only drawback is that Abbott, English and Hancock Lakes are prettier and closer to the main trail.

Two miles (and two more river crossings), beyond the Lake of the Island turnoff, at the meadowed flat just above the remains of Abbott Cabin, you'll find a four-way junction, with the faint Abbott Lake Trail taking off south and the Big Meadows/Bug Gulch Trail heading north. Although the valley widens here, the path feels much more mountainous than the lower trail, with more open forests, many wildflowers and abundant Sadler oak.

Abbott Lake is worth a visit, although it requires still another river crossing. The rocky, one mile path climbs like mad, from 4800 feet to 5700 feet, to an eight acre lake in a tight cirque with a steep headwall. The lake is 20 feet deep and contains brook trout.

The Big Meadows/Bug Gulch Trail, heading north from Abbott Cabin, bears exploration if you have tons of time. Obviously, this is not the same Big Meadows as described in Chapter 4.

From the cabin site, it's three steep, winding miles up the BM/BG Trail, and a side trail, to Horse Range Lake (3½ acres, eight feet deep, 6000 feet, rainbow trout), and four steeper and more winding miles to Wild Lake (3½ acres, 5400 feet, 24 feet deep, brook and rainbow), Ethel Lake (nine acres, 5700 feet, 22 feet deep, brook trout), Katherine Lake (five acres, 5800 feet, 13 feet deep, brook and rainbow trout), and Big Meadows (a silted-in marsh inside a pretty little cirque, near Wild Lake). These places involve a number of side trails so visiting them all entails far more than just four miles there and back.

A mile above Abbott Cabin, at mile 11, the trail begins its ascent of English Peak, breaking out onto granitic rock and much more open terrain. See the Hancock Lake section to learn what there is to see.

The Little North Fork Trail: Really long and really steep

Although Brian Boothby and I hiked the Little North Fork Trail in the downriver direction, on the way home from Garden Gulch, I shall describe it upstream from the trailhead. Hikers should carry the current (1990 or later) Marble Mountain Wilderness Map. Since the trail was drastically rerouted after the 1987 forest fires, the 1987 Wilderness map and the 1988 Klamath National Forest map shows it incorrectly.

A road indicated on the 1990 map theoretically cuts six miles off the route. The long-closed route was re-opened in 1987 to reach a fire at Devil's Canyon. While they later improved the road's first couple miles to accommodate a logging operation, the hastily constructed final miles have since collapsed. Even if you made it to the road end, it is questionable if you could find your way to the trail. The road is gated, anyhow. A perfectly good road does intersect the trail near Specimen Creek. Were it not also gated, it would whack two miles off the trail.

From the trailhead, the path wends its way through the woods, high above the river. After a mile, it picks up an old ditch, which it follows for an easy, shaded, totally level second mile. It felt to me like far more than two miles to Specimen Creek, despite the sign at the trailhead. But then, we were tired from two days backpacking and anxious to get home.

You don't actually see the Little North Fork until just past Sur Cree Creek, three miles up. There, the trail drops abruptly to the water, fords it, follows the bank for ¼ mile, then climbs several hundred feet up the far bank. During high water, this would be the end of your trip.

A half mile after scaling the far bank, the trail drops briefly to the river again before resuming its trek through the woods, high up the canyon's east slope. You don't touch water again until the crossing of the Uncles Creek, at the Wilderness boundary, five miles from the trailhead. Uncles Creek is a beautiful, shaded respite with much water.

Hasty, last minute note: In september, 1994, a 7000 acre fire burned much of the Specimen Creek drainage. And yes, it impacted the Little North Fork Trail, between the river crossing and Uncles Creek. Burns adjacent to the trail, however, were not very hot and did little damage. Higher up, the situation was far, far worse.

The next landmark after Uncles Creek is Timber Hotel, a wooded flat near the river, 1½ miles past the Right Hand Fork. While it's a fine campsite, not much else distinguishes it. The name "Timber Hotel" is a joke, referring to the fact that you are sleeping under the trees.

A half-mile past Timber Hotel, the path inscribes a wide "U" through Snowslide Gulch, an impressive rushing stream with several tiers of waterfalls.

Within ¾ mile, beginning ¼ mile before Snowslide Gulch, you come to: (1) the first Snowslide Gulch cutoff, leading north to Hancock Lake, (2) Snowslide Gulch, (3) the Devil's Canyon Trail, heading south, across the river and up a side creek, (4) the second Snowslide Gulch cutoff, also leading north to Hancock Lake. On the map, the second cutoff to Hancock Lake appears the preferred route. It is supposedly the best constructed, with long switchbacks to take the edge off the steepness.

To reach Hancock Lake in the 13 miles advertised on the trailhead sign, follow one of the two northbound cutoffs bracketing Snowslide Gulch. Although I somehow missed the second, supposedly better one, the Forest Service assures me it exists and will get you to Hancock Lake. The first one appeared extremely steep and rather faint. However you go, the two paths unite 1½ miles up, meeting the North Fork Trail after another mile. This is the 2200 foot hill referred to earlier.

If you miss the cutoffs, aren't into toting a heavy pack up such a steep grade or aren't going directly to the Hancock Lake area, continue up the Little North Fork for three more miles, to its terminus at Hamilton Camp. Two miles past Snowslide Gulch, the path dips down to the river, then begins a series of long switchbacks. On the map, this last uphill segment appears to be a mile long, with a 1000 foot rise, most of it in the lower half. The map does not show the switchbacks, however, and it felt like much more than a mile.

Hamilton Camp, a large, eroded hillside pasture full of cows, marks the end of the Little North Fork Trail. Between Hamilton Camp and the junction with the North Fork/Garden Gulch Trail, $\frac{1}{8}$ mile away at a ridgetop saddle, the Little North Fork Trail grows somewhat faint as it crosses the pastures. You're unlikely to get lost, however. We found no water at Hamilton Camp.

Done in by Garden Gulch/Chimney Rock

It seemed like a great idea: Drive three miles past the Little North Fork trailhead, hike in on the Garden Gulch Trail and return via the Little North Fork Trail. While Garden Gulch leads to Hancock Lake in the same distance as the Little North Fork, it starts 2000 feet higher. The route would allow a peek at the supposedly outstanding Chimney Rock area. We left Brian Boothby's car at the Little North Fork trailhead and my wife drove us up to the Garden Gulch trailhead, then went home.

I knew from the map that the Garden Gulch path climbed 2400 feet in its initial $2\frac{1}{2}$ miles, to 6500 feet. I figured we'd get most of the climbing out of the way right off, then the coast the rest of the way. Besides, I'd hiked the Boulder Creek Trail (Chapter 4), a few weeks earlier, with no ill effect. It climbs 3000 feet in three miles.

I did not notice on the map that immediately beyond the ridge, the path drops 1000 feet and that you lose and make up that 1000 feet several times. I also did not factor in that I hadn't been backpacking in two years, that it was 105 degrees out, that the air was smokey from forest fires, that I'd picked up a virus and that every water source in the 13 miles to Hancock Lake, except the trickle at Ahlgren Cabin, was dry as the Mojave.

I managed to survive the initial hill. From the unmarked trailhead, the path is level for the first 100 yards. Then the fun begins as it embarks on a series of switchbacks to the wilderness boundary, a mile away. The trailhead is marked by an enamel sign ¼ mile up. The path is well trodden and easy to follow, although 99% of its use is by cattle.

Two miles up, after a zillion switchbacks through a middle elevation woods (Douglas-fir, white pine, white fir, tanoak, golden chikapin), the route passes Mud Lake, an unstocked pond far below in a small meadow. Soon after, the path breaks into the open, making its way up an exposed slope of grass and mountain mahogany, to Yellow Jacket Ridge. We'd drained our canteens by then in the smokey heat, but the map showed water at Ahlgren Cabin, Crapo Meadows and numerous locations between Crapo Meadows and Hamilton Camp. We planned to spend the night at either Crapo Meadows, seven miles in, or Hamilton Camp, nine miles in.

Beyond the summit, the path drops down a series of pretty, if heavily grazed, meadowed benches for a mile, then heads into the woods for another mile, bottoming out at mile 4½, a half-mile before Ahlgren Cabin. After all that initial climbing, I found myself unable to negotiate an easy 200 foot rise in the final half mile to the cabin.

I can shake off a lot when backpacking; extreme fatigue, sore muscles, shortness of breath, blisters, orthopedic pain, twisted ankles, headache, etc. The one impossible thing to ignore is nausea. Three minutes after its onset, I dropped my pack and ended up lying on the trail moaning for nearly an hour. We limped into Ahlgren Cabin, where we decided to spend the night.

Ahlgren Cabin turned out to be delightful, with pastures, feed barn, corral, water trough and a locked cabin. Crapo Creek, running past the cabin, was the meagerest of trickles but sufficient to fill our canteens. A spigot by the water trough takes water directly from the creek. I later learned that the area is supposedly rife with giardia.

Shortly after Ahlgren Cabin, the trail climbs to a low saddle with the first view of Chimney Rock, English Peak and, thousands of feet below, the Little North Fork headwaters. The region is an immense, lakeless, white granite glacial basin, capped by Chimney Rock, a pyramidal spire only slightly higher than the adjacent jagged ridge. From what I could see, there is nothing chimneyesque about it.

From the saddle, the path follows the ridge line uphill through a sparse, high elevation woods, to the junction with the Crapo Meadows Trail. The junction lies at 6400 feet, 800 feet above and 1½ miles beyond Ahlgren Cabin. Chimney Rock rises immediately overhead, to 6873 feet.

On the Crapo Meadows Trail, it's a half-mile to Crapo Meadows and a great view of the Trinity Alps. There is usually water at the meadows but you have to hunt for it. A mile farther down the Crapo Trail, at the junction with the Portuguese Peak/Steinacher Creek Trail (Chapter 9), you come to the headwall above seldom visited Steinacher Lake, a lush, grass fringed pool on a level flat. The lake, at 5800 feet elevation, covers 2½ acres, plunges to a depth of five feet and contains brook and rainbow trout.

In the vicinity is Chimney Rock Lake, in a pocket northeast of and 300 feet above Steinacher Lake. Follow the barren ridge above Steinacher Lake, off the trail, towards Chimney Rock. You should pick up a way trail. Chimney Rock Lake covers 5½ acres at 6300 feet, in a steep, rocky basin atop a level bench. The shore is wooded near the outlet, with excellent campsites. The lake is 22 feet deep and contains rainbow and brook trout. Chimney Rock forms the lake's headwall.

The Crapo Trail ends eight miles from the Garden Gulch junction, on a short spur road at the mouth of Crapo Creek, on the Salmon River, four miles below Forks of Salmon.

Back on the Garden Gulch Trail, beyond the Crapo Meadows junction, the route gradually drops (400 feet in 1½ miles), to Hamilton Camp. For the first time, it gets into scenery worth backpacking into a Wilderness to see (although it's not nearly as impressive as English Peak/Hancock Lake).

The trail winds through a picturesque rock garden containing every wildflower imaginable, with white granite outcroppings, emerald meadows, numerous springs and small creeks, and stunted mountain hemlocks with bent, goblin tops. I have never seen Indian paintbrush as tall, as deeply red or in clusters as massive.

I should add that despite evidence of much flowing water, including caked mud, water bars and moist-site plants such as corn lily and monkshood, absolutely everything was dried up.

A half-mile before Hamilton Camp, a 1¼ mile side trail takes off to Clear Lake. The side path rises 400 feet, then drops 1000 feet, down a steep headwall, to a granite basin on a bench overlooking the Wooley Creek drainage. Although the basin is mostly rocky and barren, the somewhat brushy shore has many wooded spots with good campsites. The lake covers 6½ acres at 5400 feet, with a depth of 62 feet (six feet shallower than Deep Lake). Fishing for brook, rainbow and brown trout is said to be outstanding. And yes, the water is exceptionally clear.

Just above Clear Lake, in the same basin, Lily Lake covers 2½ acres, with a depth of five feet. It is choked with pond lilies and not regularly stocked.

Where the Clear Lake trail hits the ridge and begins a long switchback down to the lake, you should find a way trail north to Lost Lake, a half-mile distant. Lost Lake covers eight acres at 5650' elevation. It is 30 feet deep and stocked with brook, rainbow and brown trout. There are a few campsites back in the woods, away from the brushy shore.

The pretty stuff ends just beyond the Clear Lake junction, when the path hits the wooded bench upon which Hamilton Camp is perched. Although there's not much to see, Hamilton Camp is a welcome respite, three miles past Ahlgren Cabin and five miles before Hancock Lake.

Because of the scarcity of water and the fact that I still wasn't feeling 100%, we cut our Garden Gulch trip short at Hamilton Camp, picking up the far end of the Little North Fork Trail there, where we were assured of water within a mile or two. Hancock Lake involved five more miles of hiking, with two more 1000 foot climbs and drops, all out in the open and with possibly no water until we reached the lake. Although there is usually water at the spring at Tom Taylor Cabin, 2½ miles away, we couldn't be sure in the extreme drought and late August heat. Reluctantly, we put off Hancock Lake for a later trip up the North Fork.

The Garden Gulch/Little North Fork debacle brings up an interesting point. We hiked 20 miles in two days, during which we encountered only one mile of really good scenery. And that mile wasn't as scenic as many other areas of the Marble Mountain. We visited no lakes, took no pictures and were pretty much exhausted and miserable most of the time.

Here's the question: Did we have a good time?—You bet we did.

The payoff: Hancock Lake/English Peak

English Peak, elevation 7350 feet, is the highest point in a granitic pluton in the south central Marble Mountains. Hancock Lake, two miles from and 1000 feet below English Peak, is the third largest in the Marbles, after Ukonom and Cliff Lakes. Some say it's the most beautiful, set in a sprawling basin of white granodiorite and bright orange serpentine.

Of the three largest lakes, Hancock is by far the most difficult to reach. Cliff Lake (Chapter 5), is a five mile day-hike. The shortest route to Ukonom Lake (Chapter 9), involves a grueling, seven mile, two day trip. For Hancock Lake, allow at least three days. The shortest route covers 13 miles, with several ups and downs in excess of 1000 to 2000 feet. The experience, while not easy, will be memorable.

Hancock Lake is not the Marbles' most remote spot accessible by trail. That honor goes to the area along Wooley Creek (Chapter 8), between North Fork and Anthony Milne Camps, 15 miles from the Wooley Creek trailhead and 10 miles from Marble Valley. You can reach it from the North Fork Trail, via Big Meadows Creek, past Wild Lake. It's a seven mile side trip, one way.

Soon after the Abbott Lake turnoff, on the North Fork Trail headed west towards Hancock Lake, the path ascends 2000 feet in three miles, up a glacially scoured granite gorge, to 6900 feet at Diamond Lake. Though far from a pushover, this is a much easier grade than the worst sections of the Little North Fork or Garden Gulch Trails.

The next stop, 1½ miles above Abbott Cabin, is English Lake, ¼ mile from the trail in a deep, symmetrical basin reminiscent of the Rose Bowl. A large moraine, blocking the outlet, heightens the bowl effect. English Lake covers 6½ acres at 5750 feet. It is 28 feet deep and contains brook trout. Several campsites line its wooded shore. Upper English Lake, immediately above the main Lake, covers one acre and is five feet deep. It is also a brook trout haven.

After another mile of climbing, up an impressive white slope with long vistas of English Lake and the North Fork, the trail crests at Diamond Lake, where the Hancock Lake Trail comes in from the north. Diamond Lake is a half-acre pond with no fish but some good campsites in its grass and rock ledge shore.

From the Diamond Lake junction, it's one mile, and a 600 foot drop, to Hancock Lake. As at Ukonom Lake, the lake does not nestle against the basin headwall. Instead, there is a sizeable upper valley of woods and meadow. The lake and upper valley are surrounded by three 7000 foot peaks, all sculpted by the same glacier which produced the lake. Hancock Lake covers 44 acres at an elevation of 6350 feet. It is 56 feet deep and contains large brook, rainbow and brown trout.

The lake's outlet lies on the north side, where a saddle overlooks the main valley of Hancock Creek, with its meadows, cliffs and barren rock slopes. Hancock Lake occupies what geologists call a "hanging valley" above Hancock Creek. The lake drains spectacularly over a rock ledge, down the cliffs and into the lower valley. The lower valley is a barren, lakeless cirque, carved by a glacier which cut headword into the Hancock Lake basin and probably captured its outflow from Tobacco Creek.

The low spot on the lake's west shore, which descends gradually through a forested pocket into Tobacco Creek, looks like the more natural outlet and probably once was. Tobacco Lake, a fishless pond, likes down the hill, ½ mile away.

Little Hancock Lake can be reached via a short side trail from the Hancock Lake Trail. It covers one acre, in the rocks 400 feet above Hancock Lake. The 12 foot deep pool is home to a few brook trout.

Look for relic stands of Pacific silver fir between Diamond and Hancock Lakes. A dominant species in the middle elevations of the Cascades, north of Crater Lake, this is its southernmost occurrence. Like subalpine fir, the species has a habit of turning up in isolated clusters well outside its normal range. I had the honor of discovering one such cluster, on a trail in the Oregon Coast Range, between Grants Pass and Gold Beach. The Forest Service was impressed. Other relic Pacific silver fir stands occur near Ukonom Lake (Chapter 9) and Sugar Creek (Chapter 13).

Continuing up the North Fork Trail from Diamond Lake, the path climbs steeply for a half-mile, to a saddle above Tom's Lake (1½ acres, 6800 feet, 15 feet deep, brook and rainbow trout). It then crosses a rise to yet another saddle, at 7000 feet. There, a side trail leads to the English Peak Lookout, on a rock outcropping less than a half-mile away.

The view from the lookout is fantastic. Most prominent are Mount Shasta to the northeast, the Trinity Alps to the south and the sweeping canyon of the North Fork to the east. Look also for Medicine and Tickner Mountains to the northwest (Chapter 9); Preston Peak in the Siskiyou Wilderness to the west; Chimney Rock, Crapo Peak and the Russian Mountains to the south; and the Boulder Peak (Chapter 4), Shackleford Creek cluster (Chapter 5) to the northeast. While you can see the Marble Rim (Chapter 3), the angle is such that none of the marble is visible.

The region's final landmark rears its head a mile past the English Peak turnoff and shortly beyond Tom Taylor Cabin, built in 1940, where a one mile side trail drops 500 feet to Pine Lake. There should be water at the locked cabin. If you're not laked out, Pine Lake covers 3½ acres in a pretty little cirque at 6300 feet. The lake is 23 feet deep and contains brook and rainbow trout. A couple of small campsites dot its wooded shore.

A quarter mile past the Pine Lake turnoff, and two miles before Hamilton Camp, the Snowslide Gulch Trail intersects the main trail. If exiting via the Little North Fork, this is the path to take.

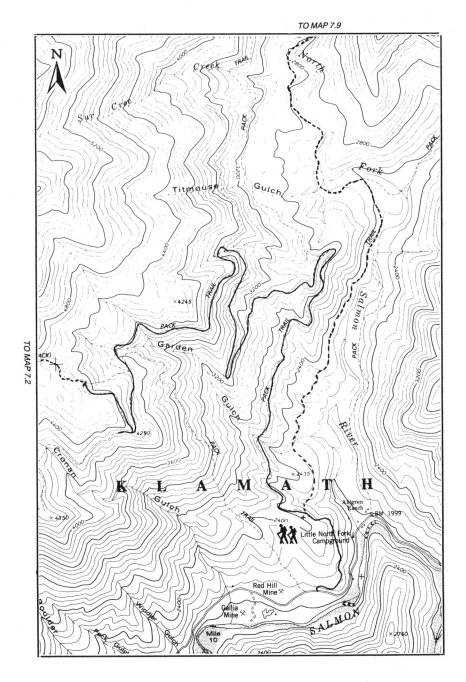

Map 7.1

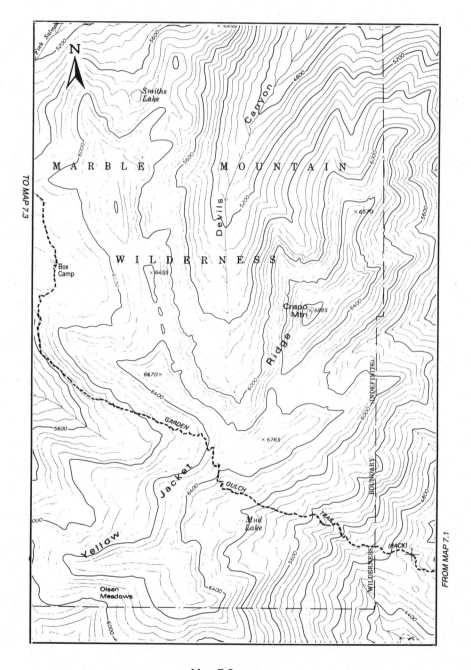

Map 7.2

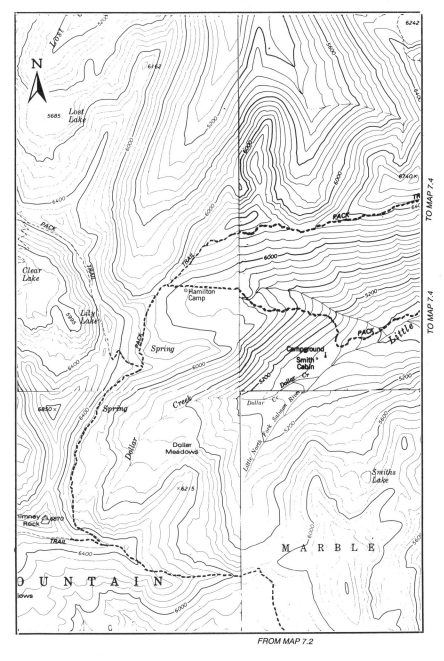

Map 7.3

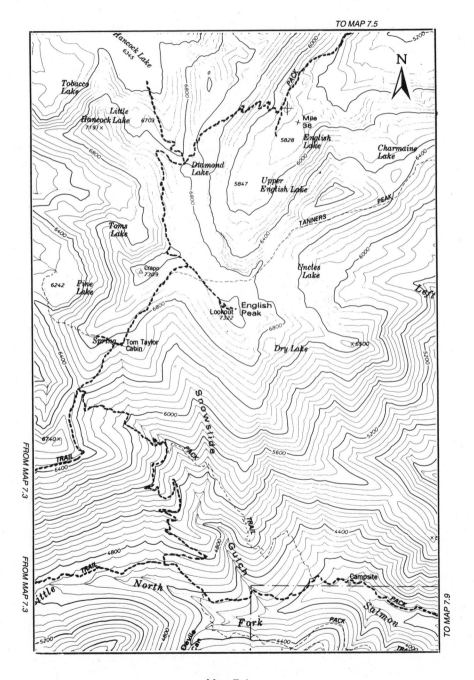

Map 7.4

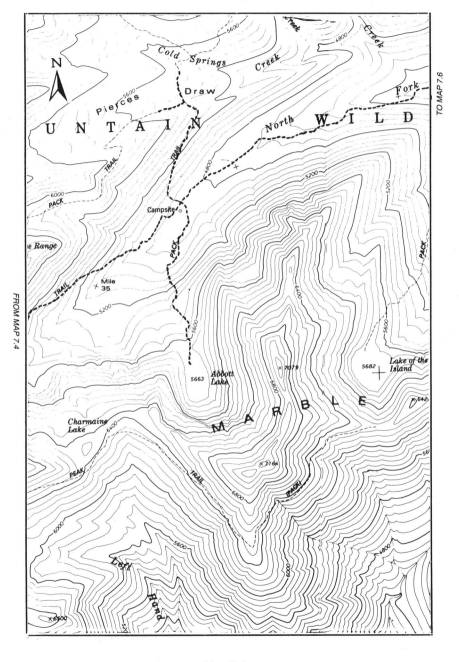

Map 7.5

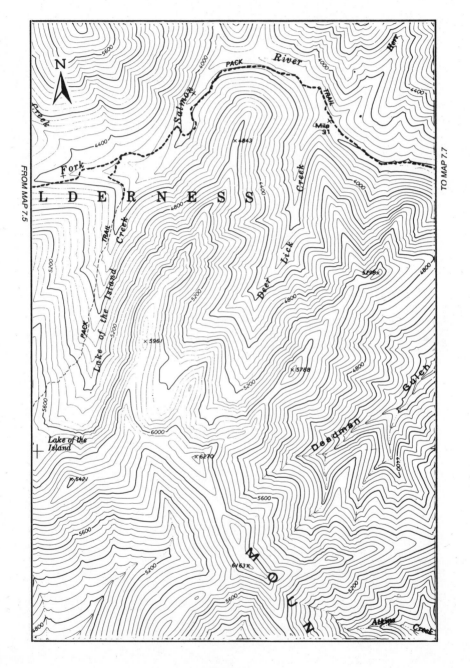

Map 7.6

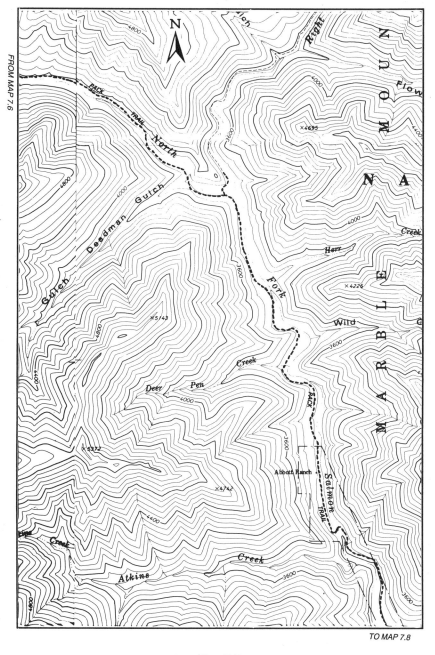

Map 7.7

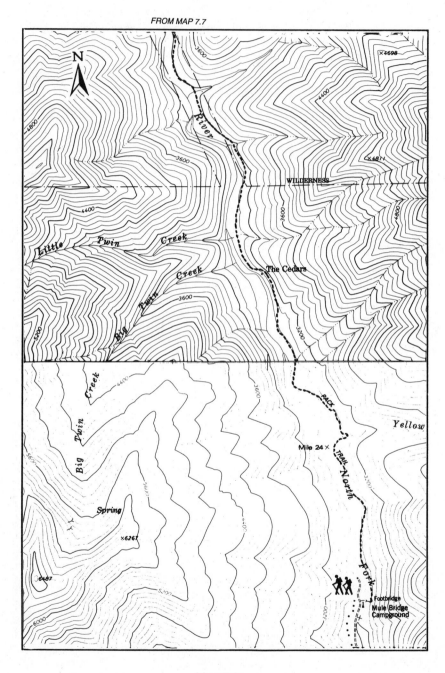

Map 7.8

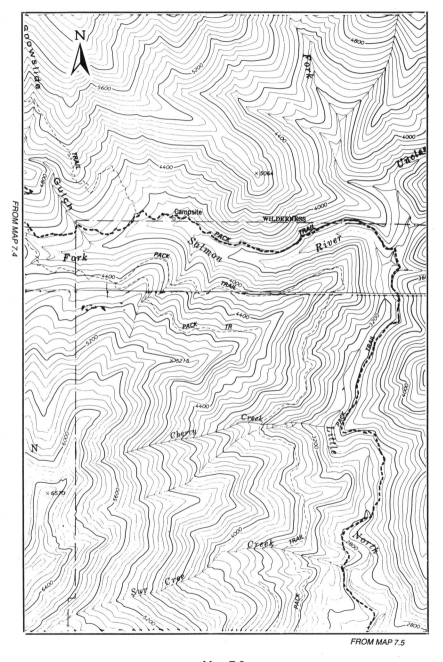

Map 7.9

8.

WOOLEY CREEK

Destinations:	Wooley Creek, Wooley Camp, Bridge Creek, Bear Skull Camp, North Fork Camp, Big Meadows Creek, Anthony Milne Camp, Ananais Camp, Big Elk Lake, Portuguese Peak.
Length:	2 miles (Wooley Creek)
	6 miles (Wooley Camp)
	14 miles (North Fork Camp)
	20 miles (Anthony Milne Camp)
	22 miles (Ukonom Lake)
	24½ miles (Big Elk Lake)
	27 miles (Marble Valley)
	40 miles (Wooley/Big Meadows/ Portuguese loop)
Difficulty:	Mostly easy but looooong
Elevation:	600 to 1200 feet (Wooley Camp)
	1800 feet (North Fork Camp)
	2600 feet (Milne Camp)
	6050 feet (Big Elk Lake)
	6200 feet (Rim above Marble Valley)
	3200 feet (Portuguese trailhead)
	5670 feet (Portuguese Peak)
Season:	All seasons
Location:	T11N-R6E-Sector 6
Water:	Plentiful
USGS 7.5" topo:	Somesbar, Medicine Mountain, English Peak, Marble Mountain
Ownership:	Klamath National Forest

Phone:	(916) 627-3291
Camping:	Oak Bottom CG
Use intensity:	Moderate to light

Directions: From I-5, north of Yreka, take Highway-96 past Happy Camp to Somesbar. At Somesbar, turn left onto the Salmon River Road. It's two miles to Oak Bottom Campground and three to the large, well marked Wooley Creek trailhead. The lower parking area is for Salmon River access and the upper is for the Wooley Creek Trail. See text for directions to the Portuguese Peak trailhead.

Wooley wooley

For those interested in really, I mean <u>really</u>, getting into the Wilderness, few California trails are as long or utterly remote as the Wooley Creek Trail. Use, though classified as "light" in the upper portions, is surprisingly heavy considering the trailhead's location in one of California's most difficult to reach spots and the fact that the path hits no high lakes or mountain ridges for 25 miles.

The Wooley Creek drainage takes up a full ⅓ of the Marble Mountain Wilderness Area's 225,000 acres. While the trail does little besides follow along the creek, and remains well up the hillside for the first six miles, it offers some of the most exciting fishing anywhere, including summer (and winter) runs of steelhead and king salmon.

Just visiting the mouth of Wooley Creek is memorable, with its gray rock gorge and aqua waters. For a closer look, take the first left over the bridge, immediately beyond the trailhead. Also, while in the neighborhood, don't miss the drive along the Salmon River from Somesbar to Forks of Salmon, through an incredible white granite canyon. It's the same granodiorite formation as Medicine and Tickner Mountains (Chapter 9). The first 10 miles of the Wooley Creek trail crosses through this formation.

Due to low elevation, the Wooley Creek Trail is accessible year round to North Fork Camp, and well beyond if you're adventurous or it's a dry season. In mid-summer, the canyon can get quite warm. In winter, there are no bears. Summer or winter, the initial two miles, to where the trail briefly meets the creek for the first time, makes an outstanding day-hike.

Bridge over Salmon River, to mouth of Wooley Creek, from the Wooley Creek Trail

The only imposing upgrade in the first 20 miles, is the initial half-mile, which rises 600 feet in a straight shot, to 1200 feet. The 640 foot elevation at the mouth of Wooley Creek is the Wilderness Area's lowest point. The highest, Boulder Peak (8299 feet), lies 30 miles away, at the end of the Boulder Creek Trail (Chapter 4).

While the Wooley Creek Trail's first ½ mile is exceedingly steep and crosses low elevation, exposed brush fields, it's soon over. The path crests at a rock point called the "Golden Elbow," with views of the Salmon River Canyon, the rocky mouth of Wooley Creek (which is nearly as voluminous as the Salmon), two bridges and the trailhead parking lot.

Low elevation conifers include Douglas-fir, sugar pine, black and white oak, madrone, etc. Canyon liveoak thrives in the steep, thinly soiled hillsides. Wildflowers abound in spring, especially lupine and Indian paintbrush. Look also for red delphinium, pentstemon and balsamroot.

Beyond the rock point, the path levels off for 1½ miles. There are excellent views of the Salmon River at first, after which things get a little dull. The route crosses several side creeks here, with water plentiful until mid-summer.

Finally, two miles from the trailhead, the path makes a long, steep pitch, dropping 300 feet from a small crest to the bank of Wooley Creek. It's a lovely spot, with the creek making a wide sweep through a gray rock gorge. Unfortunately, the trail bottoms out 20 brushy, rocky feet up from the water. It then starts back uphill without so much as a blink. There's a campsite 1/10th mile up, with drinking water at Deer Lick Creek. A log spans the gushing creek, set in a deep ravine.

The rest of Wooley Creek

The next four miles, to Wooley Camp, differ little from the first two miles. They hug a densely wooded hillside, hundreds of feet up from the creek. A highlight is Gates Creek, a rushing series of cascades spanned by a log. Eventually, the wide, forested flat around Wooley Camp appears, although the trail remains high up the hillside, winding through the canyon of Wooley Camp Creek to avoid some private cabins. Stay left at the junction with the trail leading to the cabins.

Immediately beyond the last cabin, the path makes a "wow" through the narrow, rock gorge mouth of Haypress Creek. This is one of two foot bridges (or "Bailey bridges") on the route. Haypress Creek originates at Haypress Meadows, also accessed by one of the primary trails to Ukonom Lake (Chapter 9).

To visit, and fully appreciate, the area beyond Wooley Camp, it is best to bring stock and ride, rather than walk. This will allow you to slow down and carry more provisions than otherwise. See this chapter's final section for a 40 mile horse loop beginning at the Wooley Creek trailhead and exiting via Portuguese Peak.

Between Haypress Creek and Bridge Creek, the Wooley Creek Trail hugs the streamside much more closely, although it still brushes it only occasionally. This is a marvelous stretch through deep woods, with side trails leading to secluded campsites on Wooley Creek. Fishing is outstanding.

Three miles above Wooley Camp, the spectacular mouth of Bridge Creek, where a deafening waterfall crashes into a sylvan collecting pool, contains the second of the two foot bridges on the Wooley Creek route. A side path leads to a large, beautiful campsite soon after. It's ¼ mile from the creek crossing and campsite to the Bridge Creek Trail junction. A short alternate to Fowler Cabin comes up ¼ mile beyond the Bridge Creek junction.

The Bridge Creek Trail not only begins well away from the creek mouth, it doesn't come anywhere near the creek for four miles because of the rockiness of the Bridge Creek gorge. The trail leads to Ukonom Lake in 13 miles (22 miles from the Wooley Creek trailhead). This is not the best way to Ukonom Lake since it hits few highlights and runs well away from the streams. It's nine miles up the Bridge Creek trail to Cuddihy and Onemile Lakes.

The Bridge Creek Trail meets Bridge Creek at an old growth stand containing some of the largest Douglas-firs in the Wilderness. This unique site also contains the tallest golden chinkapin trees known to exist. It is interesting that while white fir is the usual climax species at these elevations, Douglas-fir appears to be maintaining a stable state of dominance.

After a short climb in and out of Canyon Creek (not the same Canyon Creek as Chapter 3), the Wooley Creek Trail continues its upstream march. Watch for the granitic boulders to gradually disappear as the parent rock becomes metavolcanic (by "disappearing boulders," I don't mean...). Anyhow, soon after, Wooley Creek tumbles down a series of rock bench waterfalls.

Four miles beyond the Bridge Creek junction, the open, grassy flat of Bear Skull Camp appears, with North Fork Camp showing up a mile beyond. The bear skull which used to mark Bear Skull Camp is long gone. The canyon narrows a little as it approaches Bear Skull Camp, then widens at the mouth of the North Fork. As noted, the North Fork has no trail access. To visit its headwaters, follow the Marble Rim Trail from Four Corners above Marble Valley, towards the Rainy Lake access trail (Chapter 3).

A log spans the mouth of the North Fork, at North Fork Camp. Hopefully, it's still there, although this trail section isn't maintained very often. Another campsite, beside a beautiful, deep pool, turns up ¾ mile upstream from North Fork Camp.

The five miles between North Fork Camp and Anthony Milne Camp, crosses the dead center of the wilderness and is the most remote segment of the Marbles' most remote trail. You're still under 3000 feet elevation, the woods are lovely, dark and deep, and the fishing remains outstanding. You may encounter some faint spots in the trail, however.

The major point of interest in this segment is the Big Meadows Trail. Heretofore, the path has confined itself to the creek's north bank. In the half-mile around the Big Meadows Trail junction, the Wooley Creek Trail crosses Wooley Creek, crosses Big Meadows Creek, passes the Big Meadows Trail turnoff, then crosses Wooley Creek three more times before resuming its accustomed position on the north bank. These are all boulder hops. The Forest Service plans to rework this section, keeping the trail entirely on the north shore.

The Big Meadows Trail hits Wild Lake and Big Meadows in five miles and the North Fork (of the Salmon) Trail in eight miles (Chapter 7). Big Meadows, in a tiny, lakeless glacial cirque, while truly lovely, isn't all that big. Nor is it the same Big Meadows described in Chapter 3. Not by a long shot.

Anthony Milne Camp marks the confluence of Wooley Creek and the South Fork of Wooley Creek. The South Fork begins at Wooley Lake while the main fork commences at Maneaten Lake. Both lakes are best accessed via Kidder Creek (Chapter 6). There is no trail up the South Fork or up Wooley Creek above Anthony Milne Camp.

Above Anthony Milne, the path begins climbing at a moderate to steep clip, hugging a hillside several hundred feet above the water as it gradually pulls away from Wooley Creek and into the Big Elk Creek drainage. From an elevation of 2600 feet at Milne Camp, the trail makes its way through the woods and past some rocky openings, to 4800 feet at Wooley Pocket, three miles away. Wooley Pocket is the steepest, deepest and last of a number of steep, deep side creeks spanned by this section of trail.

Wooley Pocket is a charming little campsite with some delicious springs immediately beyond. Above the pocket, the trail levels for 1 ½ miles, hitting Big Elk Creek for the first time, then crossing it, in the meadows around Ananais Camp. A short trail right, immediately across the creek, leads to the camp and its gushing artesian spring. From Ananais Camp (5000 feet), it's 1½ miles to Big Elk Lake (6000 feet) and two miles to Four Corners Saddle (6200 feet), a mile from Marble Valley (6000 feet).

Son, that's a powerful lot of walking.

The long way home: Portuguese Peak

What makes the Portuguese Peak Trail so attractive is that its trail-head lies very near the Wooley Creek trailhead. For purists desiring to wander the Wilderness for weeks on end, never running into anybody and never retracing their steps, the Wooley Creek/Portuguese Peak loop is outstanding.

Portuguese Peak is named for the many early settlers in the Scott Valley/Salmon River area who came from Portugal. They and their descendants are marvelous people who have contributed much to the region's richness and diversity.

As for extended trips into the Wilderness, if you want to really go nuts, enter the Marbles via Kidder Creek, take the PCT from above Kidder Lake to Four Corners, near Marble Valley, hike across to Cuddihy Lakes, follow the Bridge Creek Trail to Wooley Creek, go up Wooley Creek to the Big Meadows Trail, take Big Meadows to the North Fork Trail, follow the North Fork to the Right Hand Fork and take it to the Shelly Fork trailhead. Such a route would cover well over 1000 miles (actually, more like 60).

The 40 mile Portuguese Peak loop begins at the Wooley Creek trailhead, goes 20 miles up Wooley Creek to Big Meadows Creek, follows the Big Meadows Trail to the North Fork, takes the North Fork Trail past Hancock Lake and Chimney Rock to the Crapo Mead-ows Trail, then picks up the Portuguese Peak Trail a mile later, above Steinacher Lake (Chapter 7). This is a fairly popular horse route.

While the Wooley Creek trailhead is only a mile down the road from the turnoff to the Portuguese Peak trailhead, the actual trail-heads are six miles apart. That's because the Portuguese Peak access road is five miles long. So unless you arrange a pickup, the loop is really 46 miles. To reach the Portuguese Peak trailhead, continue east from the Wooley Creek trailhead to road 12N01, on the left. Follow signs to the Steinacher Creek Trail. Head up 12N01 to the trailhead, which is very much oriented towards stock use.

Although it doesn't compare to the best of the Marbles, the first part of the Portuguese Peak Trail makes a decent day-hike. It's 3½ miles to Portuguese Peak, climbing from 3200 feet to 5700 feet. Views of Wooley and Steinacher Creeks, the Salmon River, the Trinity Alps and the Marbles abound, especially from the top of Portuguese Peak.

From the trailhead to a mile past Portuguese Peak, the path follows the top of the ridge forming the Wilderness area's south boundary. The first 1½ miles are exceedingly steep, even for the Marbles, gaining 1700 feet as the trail switches back and forth up the fire scarred ridge. Note the contrast between north and south slopes, with north slopes much more densely forested and south slopes brushy and open, with much manzanita.

Things level off in the vicinity of Tom Payne Peak, a 5098 foot knoll which the trail just misses to the north. Was this the same Payne for whom Paynes Lake was named? Can I resist a remark about the trail being a Payne?

Immediately beyond Tom Payne Peak, the path drops 400 feet, levels off for a mile, drops a little more, pushes through some brush patches (mostly thimbleberry), then begins yet another serious climb. Things become really hot and brushy here (like they weren't before), as the path moves out onto crumbly rock. The final mile gains 1000 feet in a series of wildflower and brush choked switchbacks, to a point just north of Portuguese Peak's 5670 foot summit. A short way trail accesses the summit.

Beyond Portuguese Peak, the path climbs 800 feet two miles, enters the English Peak granitic area, then pretty much levels off until Hamilton Camp.

Son, that's a powerful lot of horseback riding.

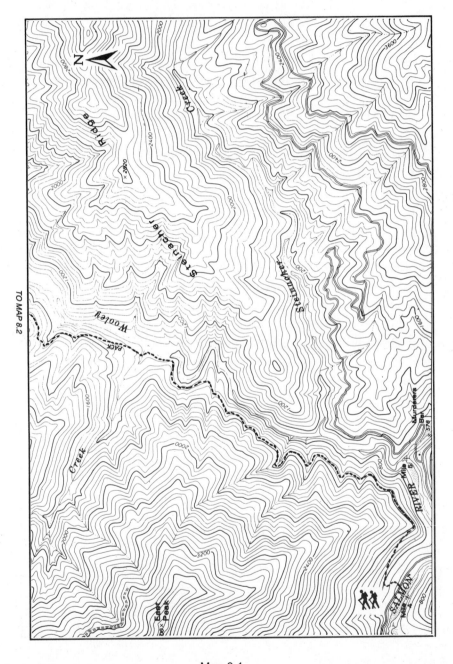

Map 8.1

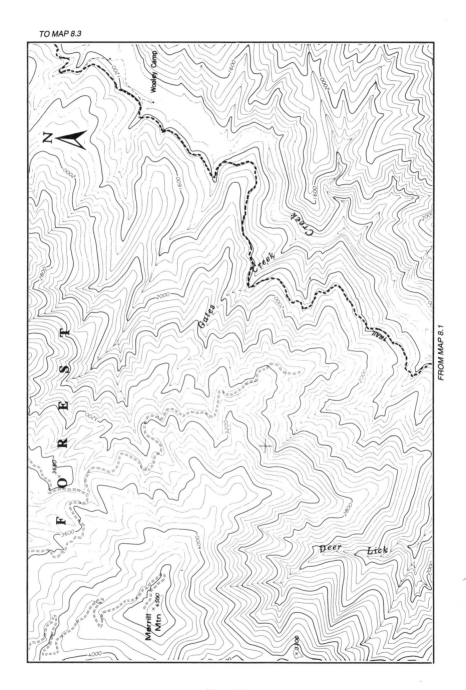

Map 8.2

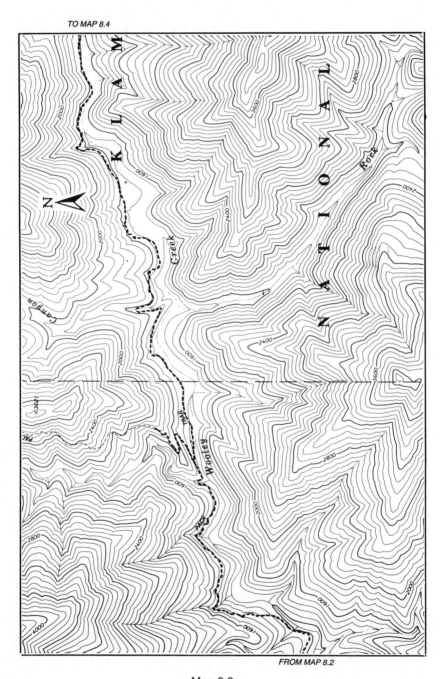

Map 8.3

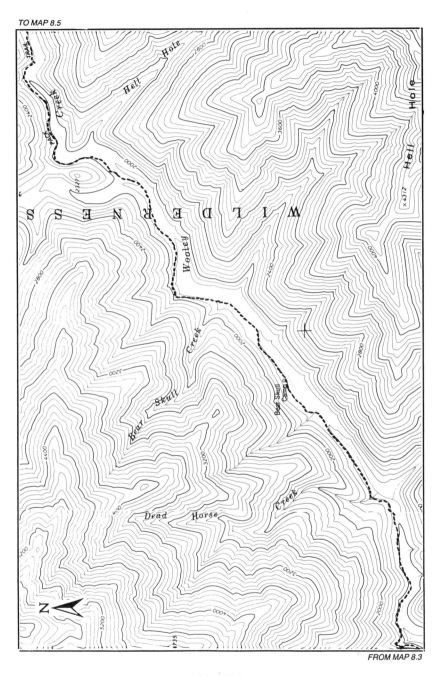

Map 8.4

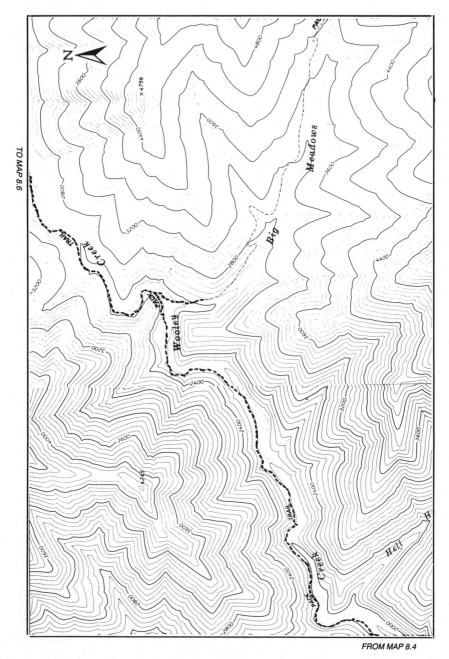

TO MAP 8.6

FROM MAP 8.4

Map 8.5

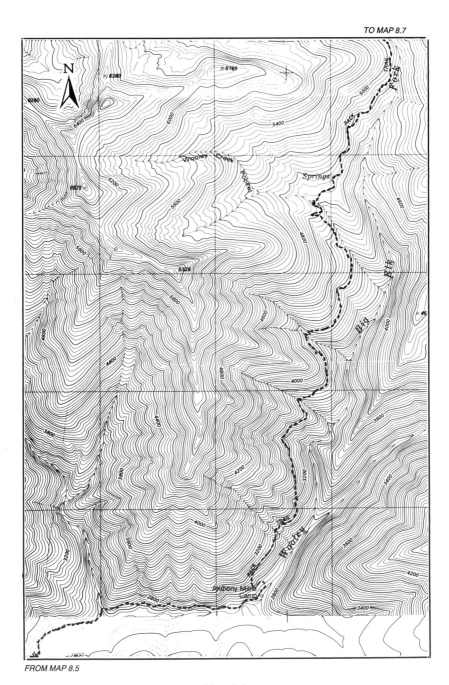

TO MAP 8.7

FROM MAP 8.5

Map 8.6

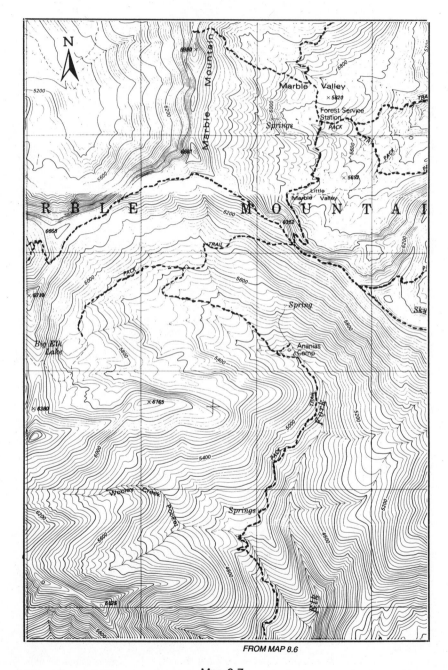

FROM MAP 8.6

Map 8.7

9.

UKONOM LAKE

Destinations:	Johnson Hunting Ground, Tickner Hole, Tickner Lake, Snyder Lake, Ukonom Lake, Independence Lake, Cuddihy Lakes, Blue Granite Lake, Green Granite Lake, Gold Granite Lake, Onemile Lake, Secret Lake, Deadman Lake, Pleasant Lake, Meteor Lake, McCash Lake, Hooligan Lake, Medicine Mountain, Monument Lake, Pickle Camp, Round Meadow, Haypress Meadows.
Length:	miles (Ukonom via Johnson) 9 miles (Cuddihy via Johnson or Haypress) 4½ miles (Pickle Camp via Haypress) 11 miles (Ukonom via Haypress)
Water:	Enough
Season:	June through October
Difficulty:	Difficult (Johnson) Moderate (Haypress)
Elevation:	5600 feet (Johnson TH) 6400 feet (Johnson Hunting Ground) 5300 feet (Tickner Hole) 6800 feet (Tickner crest) 6050 feet (Ukonom Lake) 4400 feet (Haypress TH) 6500 feet (Height of Haypress Tr.) 6837 feet (Medicine Mountain) 5700 feet (Onemile Lake) 5700 feet (Cuddihy Lake)

USGS 7.5" topo:	Ukonom Lake, Somesbar, Ukonom Mountain
	Location: T14N-R7E-Sector 2 (Johnson TH)
	T13N-R7E-Sector Sector 32 (Haypress TH)
Use intensity:	Moderate to light
Camping:	Sulphur Springs
Phone:	(916) 493-2243 (Happy Camp)
	(916) 627-3291 (Ukonom)

Directions: Johnson Hunting Ground. From I-5, 12 miles north of Yreka, follow Highway-96 to Happy Camp. Elk Creek Road takes off left at the west end of town. Follow it across the Klamath and up Elk Creek, towards Sulphur Springs. Where the road crosses Elk Creek a second time, continue straight, up a gravel road marked "Johnson Hunting Ground," instead of crossing the bridge. This is road 15N08, which eventually becomes 15N13. Continue to a saddle amid a huge area of burns and clearcuts. Follow the excellent road as it makes long switchbacks up the hill to the 10 car trailhead. Haypress Meadows. Proceed west, past Happy Camp, to Somesbar. Turn left on the Salmon River Road, towards Forks of Salmon. Immediately after, Forest Road 15N17 takes off uphill (the map says "Road 88," but I saw no such marking), towards Camp Three and "Wilderness Trails." Signs higher up say "Haypress Trail." It's 15 miles, of which the first six are one lane blacktop and the last nine are good gravel, to the main trailhead designed for heavy use by horse trailers. See text for a discussion of the alternative Let'er Buck (Black Mountain) and Stanshaw Meadows trailheads.

❖　❖　❖

Ukonom Lake: A 24 year quest

To residents of Scott Valley and the Klamath River, the Marble Mountain Wilderness is an overwhelming presence. Thus, when I moved to Scott Valley from Michigan in 1970, it didn't take long to hear about it. The first three hiking destinations recommended to me were, (1) Hidden Lake, (2) the Marble Valley, and (3) Ukonom Lake.

Hidden Lake, near Callahan Summit, is the valley's easiest high mountain lake to reach, with a paved access road and a level, 1½ mile path through a maze of steep-walled glacial cirques. It's now part of the Trinity Alps Wilderness. The Marble Valley (Chapter 3), a

4½ mile day-hike from a trailhead near Fort Jones, made the list because it may be the most beautiful place on Earth. I made it to Hidden Lake within a week of moving to Scott Valley and to Marble Valley within a month. It wasn't until 24 years later, August 24, 1994 to be exact, before I finally laid eyes on Ukonom Lake.

Ukonom Lake has many things going for it, aside from great fishing and a magnificent setting. At 67 acres, it is the largest lake in the Marble Mountains. The runner-up, Cliff Lake, in the Shackleford Creek drainage (Chapter 5), covers only 52 acres. Ukonom is the second largest natural lake in the entire Klamath Mountains system, after the dazzling Caribou Lake (72 acres), high in the Trinity Alps at the end of an 11 mile trail.

Kalamath River near Somersbar

In 1970, the shortest route to Ukonom Lake was the Jacobs Ladder Trail, off Independence Creek between Happy Camp and Somesbar. The path rose from 3200 feet at the trailhead to the 6050 foot elevation lake in 3½ miles. I started up it in 1971, on my lunch hour while working for the California Fish and Game Department, but turned back after a mile for lack of time. In 1994, the Jacobs Ladder Trail failed to appear on any map and the road to it was omitted from the Marble Mountain Wilderness map. The explanation, by the only Forest Service employee who remembered that far back, was that they deactivated the trail because of overuse at the lake.

Being somewhat of a packrat, I'd saved my 1970 map and I used it to locate the old trailhead site. The spot, I discovered, was clearcut in 1974 and the trailhead is now a logging landing. The path's initial pitch is choked with young Douglas-fir, tanoak brush and blackberry vines. I fought my way up through the steep brambles, finding no trace of a trail and feeling like the prince in the Sleeping Beauty. At the top of the clearcut, beneath a much older forest stand, the path magically appeared. While I was able to follow it, there were downed trees everywhere and large patches of impenetrable brush. Again, I got about a mile.

The time had come, I concluded, to quit looking for shortcuts and do it right.

The rise and fall of Johnson Hunting Ground

These days, the shortest route to Ukonom Lake is the Johnson Hunting Ground Trail, a seven mile trek infamous for ascending, then dropping thousands of feet every couple miles. Prior to 1987, the trail began in the deep woods at 4600 feet elevation. In that year, the Klamath River region was hit by some of the worst fires in West Coast history. Massive blazes continued for months, devastating hundreds of thousands of acres. The impact is most evident in the Kelsey Creek area (Chapter 1) and at Ukonom Lake. Entire drainages around the Johnson Hunting Ground trailhead burned, with vast areas later salvage logged. The upshot was that they extended the trailhead road to the Wilderness boundary, with a new trailhead 1000 feet higher than the old, at 5600 feet.

The path still offers a pretty fair workout. It rises 800 feet in the first two miles, plummets 1100 feet in the third mile, climbs 1400 in the next three miles, and drops 700 feet in the final mile to the lake. For backpackers, no matter how hard you try, the prospect of climbing back up that 1100 foot hill never quite goes away.

From the trailhead, the initial ¼ mile follows a closed, nearly level road to the wilderness boundary. There, the trail takes off uphill in a series of zig-zag switchbacks, through a skeleton forest of grass and burned trees. Eventually, it reaches the ridgetop, levels significantly and disappears into the woods. Soon after, the way crosses the series of ridgetop outcroppings which are Johnson Hunting Ground. Look for a massive, granite mountain in the distance, ahead and to the right. That is Tickner Mountain, the complex housing Ukonom Lake.

The panorama east from Johnson Hunting Ground affords an unusual vista of the Marble Rim (Chapter 3) from the northeast. It's spectacular certain times of day. Radiating west from the Marble Rim, the jagged, cross-wilderness chain known as the Salmon Mountains can be seen, linking the Marble Rim with Tickner Mountain and containing such landmarks as Rainy Lake, Burney Lake and Blue Granite Lake.

Also from Johnson Hunting Ground, the entire Siskiyou Wilderness Area, across the Klamath to the west, can be seen. Sawtooth Ridge and Preston Peak are most prominent. On the northeast horizon, look for the orange, double humped pinnacle of Red Butte, centerpiece of the Red Buttes Wilderness.

The level ground and long panoramas quickly become a memory as the bottom falls out of the trail. In an exhausting series of short switchbacks, it drops 800 feet to a brushy saddle, then 300 more to Tickner Hole. The high point at Johnson Hunting Ground is 6400 feet. The elevation at the Tickner Hole creek crossing is 5300 feet. An unmarked side trail just before the crossing, leads to Sulphur Springs, on Elk Creek, in six miles. The elevation at Sulphur Springs is 2200 feet.

There's a nice campsite shortly beyond the Tickner Hole creek crossing. On the way home, I filled my canteen there, preparatory to climbing the hill, even though the water was barely a trickle and muddy. It was the only halfway potable water between Ukonom Lake and the trailhead, although in a less droughty year or earlier in the season, good water abounds.

The area between the creek and Tickner Lake is a major highlight. While generally steep, it is varied, beautiful and contains many level pitches. White granitic outcroppings support widely scattered white pine, red fir, mountain hemlock and Brewer spruce. Numerous seeps maintain corn lily meadows and ponds surrounded by willow and alder brush. All the ponds were dried up when I visited. The area abounds with wild-flowers, including gentian, Indian paintbrush and fireweed.

Fireweed is the trail's dominant herbaceous species. An early invader in burned areas, it likes any open area containing a little bit of moisture. Fireweed can be spectacular, with its long, spike-like stalks, purple flowers and, in late season, cottony tufts.

The Tickner Hole area culminates at Tickner Lake, alongside the trail at the foot of Tickner Peak. The normally 1½ acre pond was in sad shape in August, 1994. When full, it's nine feet deep and stocked with brook trout. Snyder Lake lies ¼ mile away. To get there, head northeast from Tickner Lake, down a narrow, rocky pocket. Snyder covers 2½ acres at 5800 feet and is stocked with rainbow trout. Unlike the other shallow ponds in the vicinity, Snyder plummets to a depth of 47 feet.

In the half-mile beyond Tickner Lake, the trail climbs 500 feet to a grassy crest at 6800 feet elevation, only 100 feet lower than Tickner Peak. If you're dying to scale Tickner Peak, follow the ridge east for ¼ mile.

Ukonom at last

Over the crest above Tickner Lake, the path enters the woods and drops steeply to the junction with the Cuddihy Lakes Trail, ⅛ mile away. Turn right for Ukonom Lake. It's a mile, and a 700 foot drop, from the crest to the lake. Before long, the trail bursts out of the woods and Ukonom Lake, the object of all this work, appears in the distance. The path levels off as it makes its way along a rock ledge, then it drops through a series of meadows to the lake, which is surrounded by lodgepole pine and mountain hemlock.

Ukonom Lake sits at the lower end of an enormous glacial basin. Rather than lapping at the base of the basin's main headwall, like most glacial lakes, the lake's upper end emerges into a wide, tree filled valley, with the headwall above that. A white, glacially carved escarpment does rise from the lakeshore's south side. Most of the trees on it burned in 1987. Fortunately, the upper valley and lake area were spared. The lake's northwest shore consists of an immense glacial moraine of jumbled rocks and boulders.

Trail meets lake at a large meadow on the north shore, just above a rocky peninsula. To comprehend the lake's size, walk around the peninsula to the much larger south arm. There's a huge meadow at the valley head above the lake. Unlike the surrounding peaks, the rocks at the lake are black schist, not white granite. Some outstanding campsites dot the lakeshore, especially near the peninsula.

When I visited, the water level was down considerably, despite a small dam at the mouth. So maybe it was only 62 acres instead of 67. It was still impressive.

And to the morons who played their boom-box until 10:30 PM, then turned it on again at 7:00 AM—I hate you for ruining my visit. To everyone else, I caution that music is inappropriate in a Wilderness Area and carries amazing distances over water in a high walled basin.

There's a little lake over the saddle to the northeast, above Ukonom Lake. To reach it, head up the hill, off the trail, ¼ mile before Ukonom Lake. You'll end up at Independence Lake, ½ mile away. Independence Lake is the largest of several small ponds at the same elevation as Ukonom Lake. It covers 1½ lily pad choked acres, reaches a depth of 10 feet and contains brook trout. If you must blast your stereo, do it there, not at Ukonom Lake.

Haypress Meadows: Ukonom's back door

The Haypress Meadows area, a jutting square comprising the Wilderness Area's westernmost land, is vastly different from the remainder of the Marble region. Amid some of Northern California's most awesome old growth, a network of intensely green meadows, including Haypress, Stanshaw, Long, Halfmoon and Round, is reached by an excellent system of loop trails. They offer some of the region's finest and most unusual day-hiking opportunities. Day-hike destinations include Haypress Meadows (2 miles), Round Meadow (3½ miles), Pickle Camp (4½ miles) and Monument Lake (6 miles).

Haypress is not only worth visiting in its own right, it provides an excellent alternate entry to Ukonom Lake and the vast lake conglomerate south of Ukonom, including Onemile and Cuddihy. It is also the most popular route to Ukonom Lake. Although four miles longer than via Johnson Hunting Ground, it's much, much easier.

Noted for botanical diversity, the Haypress area features magnificent old growth Douglas-fir, grand fir and red fir stands dotted with wet (and a few dry) meadows. The ecosystem reaches it's maximum at Long Meadows, where several endangered species enjoy the moist, grassy expanse and the meadow/forest ecotone. Away from the meadows, the prevailing understory species in the old growth is a dense, emerald carpet of vanillaleaf and thimbleberry. The most impressive old growth lies nearer the trailheads. Farther up, trees are smaller but still magnificent. Note the transition from Douglas-fir and grand fir to red fir, white fir, lodgepole pine and mountain hemlock. Brush species include Sadler oak, little wood rose, dogwood and many others.

As impressive as the Haypress Trail is, if you want to see really gigantic old growth, including record sized golden chinkapin, make your way one drainage east, to Bridge Creek, described in Chapter 8. To reach the Bridge Creek giant tree area, either (a) hike six miles up Wooley Creek, then four miles up the Bridge Creek Trail or (b) hike three miles up the Haypress Trail, then make a right onto the Cedar Flat Trail and hike another four miles to the Bridge Creek Trail.

To mitigate crowding at the Haypress trailhead complex, two alternate trailheads have been developed, Let'er Buck and Stanshaw Meadows (plus the little used Ten Bear trailhead). Let'er Buck used to be called the "hiker" trailhead, with Haypress the "horse" trailhead. To reach Let'er Buck, turn right where the sign says "Black Mountain." Proceed two miles, past the bridge over Haypress Creek, to a junction on the left. The sign is down but the post remains. The trailhead lies 200 feet up the side road, at a bulletin board. The Wilderness map shows it a mile farther up but the final road segment has been gated and the trailhead moved.

The Let'er Buck trailhead is the same elevation as the Haypress trailhead and there is plenty of parking on the shoulder. The route joins the Haypress Trail in 2½ miles while the Haypress Trail reaches the same spot in two miles. There is little difference between the two routes except that they follow opposite sides of the extremely deep ravine of Haypress Creek. The Let'er Buck trailhead features a close-up view of Medicine Mountain, second highest in the western Marbles at 6837 feet (Tickner Peak is 80 feet higher).

For the Stanshaw Meadows trailhead, continue on 15N17 past the Haypress turnoff for another 2½ miles. The trailhead is designed for stock use and 500 feet higher than Haypress or Let'er Buck. The Stanshaw Trail joins the Haypress Trail in two miles, at the same junction as the Let'er Buck Trail. It's a little more varied at the beginning than the other routes, hitting Stanshaw Meadows right off, crossing Sandy Bar Creek at Jawbone Camp, then bisecting the heart of Haypress Meadows.

From the Haypress trailhead, the path winds steeply for ¼ mile to the wilderness boundary, then levels off for 1¾ miles. According to the map, you climb 500 feet and drop 300 feet but it is barely noticeable in the cool shade and soft, even tread. After 1½ miles, the first meadow appears, an expanse of grass and corn lily with a crossing of Haypress Creek at the far end. When I visited, in early July of a very wet year with lingering snow patches, it was necessary to wade the ankle deep creek. Later in the season (or had I been more agile), I could have boulder-hopped across, or tightroped over one of the many precarious poles spanning the creek.

Beyond the crossing, it's back into the woods and over a couple low crests before emerging at another meadow at the Stanshaw/Let'er Buck junction. The intersections are slightly offset and lie 500 feet apart. There's an outstanding campsite here, in the woods just above the creek. A ¼ mile side trip on the Stanshaw Trail takes you across Haypress Creek a second time, to the largest meadow of the Haypress complex. It's impressive, as they all are, but didn't look much bigger than the two meadows already passed. The second creek crossing also involved a bit of wading when I visited.

Shortly after Stanshaw/Let'er Buck junction, heading towards Sandy Ridge, you hit the route's major hill, climbing from 4700 feet at the creek to 6200 feet at Pickle Camp, 2½ miles away. Again, I found it much gentler than the map suggested. It's ¾ mile to the tip of Let'er Buck Meadow from the Stanshaw/Let'er Buck junction. Hang a left at the meadow for McCash Lake and Torgeson Meadow and a right shortly after for Cedar Flat and Bridge Creek.

Above Let'er Buck Meadow, the path steepens as it makes its way through a somewhat more open and less gigantic forest. In a mile, look for a barely noticeable sign marking the short ($\frac{1}{10}$th mile) side path to Round Meadow. Whatever you do, don't miss Round Meadow. Unlike the other meadows, which are marshy depressions, Round Meadow is a silted in lake at the bottom of a glacial cirque. It is far larger and much more spectacular than the other meadows, with a rock ledge headwall rising up on two sides to Pickle Camp. There's a magnificent campsite at the end of the side trail, although the meadow itself, and Halfmoon Creek running through the center, are pretty much inaccessible in the marshy grass and willow/alder brush.

Beyond the Round Meadow side trail, the Haypress Trail enters a large swath of open forest and scrub (manzanita, Sadler oak), sprawled over a dome shaped mountaintop. After surmounting a low saddle, the path crosses the summit, then arrives at the waterless but shaded and beautiful Pickle Camp, at the beginning of Sandy Ridge. From Pickle Camp to Ukonom Lake, seven miles away, the trail holds a fairly level contour between 6000 and 6400 feet. Because the route mostly follows the ridgetops, there is no trailside water for several miles, although spur trails access dozens of lakes. Sandy Ridge juts off the mountaintop with Horse Pocket on one side, McCash Lake on the other and the trail in the middle. A side trail west from Pickle Camp follows the ridge above McCash Lake. There's supposed to be a couple way trails down to it. The lake covers $3\frac{1}{2}$ acres at 5400 vegetation choked feet, and supposedly houses a few rainbow trout. It is normally only three feet deep. Forget McCash Lake unless you're taking the eight mile loop from the trailhead to Pickle Camp, past McCash Lake, through Long Meadow and the main part of Haypress Meadows, then back to the trailhead.

A mile down Sandy Ridge from Pickle Camp, the ridge widens, then narrows and a short, wildflower filled side path drops to Monument Lake, 300 feet down (at 5900 feet) and $\frac{1}{2}$ mile away. The best campsite lies in the woods, halfway down the access trail, rather than at the lake's meadowed shore. The three acre pool is 13 feet deep and stocked with brook and rainbow trout. It is the most common Haypress Trail destination.

Beyond Monument Lake, the ridge widens and narrows yet again as it makes its way to the headwall above Meteor Lake. Another short ($\frac{1}{2}$ mile) side trail drops 500 feet into Meteor Lake's forested but steep basin. The lake is a $3\frac{1}{2}$ acre puddle at 5700 feet, with a depth of 11 feet and stocked with rainbow trout.

If you notice a pattern developing, there are dozens of lakes within a five mile radius of Ukonom Lake. The closer you get, the more lakes there are, culminating with Cuddihy, Onemile and Blue Granite Lakes.

Cuddihy, Onemile, Blue Granite and much, much more·

Back at the junction just past the Tickner crest, on the way to Ukonom Lake from Johnson Hunting Ground, hang a left, instead of a right, for Blue Granite, Cuddihy and Onemile Lakes. That's just for starters since Cuddihy Lake marks the core of the Wilderness Area's premiere lake concentration.

The Granite Creek Lakes come first, with a turnoff a mile from the Tickner crest junction. From a saddle between the Ukonom basin and Granite Creek, the path drops sharply but briefly down the Granite Creek side. Soon after, the long, circuitous Granite Creek Trail takes off. It's $1\frac{1}{2}$ miles down the Granite Creek Trail, and other access trails, to Green and Gold Granite Lakes and 2 $\frac{1}{2}$ miles to Blue Granite Lake, all over rocky, terraced terrain much like the Tickner Hole region.

Just for the record, this area's granite is white; not blue, green or gold. Also for the record, it isn't really granite but granodiorite. True granite is sort of grayish pink.

Green and Gold Granite Lakes lie side by side, a half-mile up a side trail. Green Granite Lake covers four acres at 5600 feet. It is 11 feet deep and contains brook and rainbow trout. Gold Granite Lake blankets two acres at the same elevation but is 14 feet deep. It too, contains brook and rainbow trout.

Back on the Granite Creek Trail, beyond the Green/Gold turnoff, the path zig-zags steeply towards Granite Creek for a half-mile, losing several hundred feet. Where it finally meets the creek, a one mile side path to Blue Granite Lake takes off, contouring through the woods, across the creek, over a level bench and past a pond to the lake. Blue Granite is one of the area's more substantial lakes. The 12 acre pool, at 5250 feet, is 28 feet deep and stocked with brook trout.

Beyond the Blue Granite Lake turnoff, the Granite Creek Trail continues dropping, levelling off at 4800 feet. As with most trails in the area, it ends up at Sulphur Springs after 10 miles.

Back on the main trail from Tickner crest (which is now the Haypress Trail along Sandy Ridge), a mile beyond the Granite Creek turnoff, the path crosses a saddle dividing Granite Creek from the Cuddihy basin, between two prominent peaks. Soon after, the main cross-wilderness trail to Marble Valley comes in from the east, holding a level contour high up the exposed mountainside. Follow it three miles and you'll end up at Burney Lake (Chapter 3). Follow it $\frac{1}{8}$ mile to the Cuddihy Lakes access trail.

The Cuddihy (pronounced "Cuddi-high") basin may be the area's scenic climax. It's much like the Tickner Hole and Blue Granite areas except more so, with a wider basin, a steeper and more convoluted headwall, more rock and fewer trees. The Cuddihy Lakes Trail drops steeply down to a large meadow with a cairn in the middle. Turn right for the lakes or continue straight, briefly, for a beautiful campsite with a pipe spring.

It's another $\frac{1}{3}$ mile to the four main lakes, three of which cling to the base of a towering cliff. All four lakes lie at 5700 feet, with the best campsites and stock pasture at the first lake (called Cuddihy #1). The $3\frac{1}{2}$ acre lake is 18 feet deep, the one acre lake is five feet deep, the main lake covers seven acres and is 20 feet deep while the $2\frac{1}{2}$ acre lake is also 20 feet deep. All contain brook trout and are surrounded by open forests and grassy shores with large boulders. Swimming is excellent.

Supposedly, a one mile trail from Cuddihy Lakes leads to Deadman Lake. Deadman Lake lies over or around the ridge to the south, in a small sub-basin off the Cuddihy basin and at the same elevation. The nine acre pool is 25 feet deep and stocked with brook trout.

Heading south once again on the main route from Tickner crest, a half-mile past the Marble Valley turnoff, the path hits the ridge between Onemile Lake and the headwaters of Bridge Creek (Chapter 8), with outstanding views of the Cuddihy Lakes. Side trails lead in both directions. A better side trail accesses Onemile Lake $\frac{1}{4}$ mile down the main trail, at the saddle.

The Bridge Creek Trail leads to Pleasant Lake in three rocky miles, with an 800 foot drop. The worst pitch comes just beyond a small pond on the access trail off the Bridge Creek Trail, where the path negotiates an incredibly steep, rocky saddle between Bridge Creek and Pleasant Lake, ¼ mile from the lake. Pleasant Lake occupies a pleasant little cirque at 5500 feet, which drains into the remote North Fork of Wooley Creek. The lakeshore is steep, rocky and sparsely wooded, with views of Black Marble Mountain and the Marble Rim. It covers nine acres and is 37 feet deep. Brook trout live in it.

There is no good route to Hooligan Lake, one basin south of Pleasant Lake. With luck, if you climb or contour around the ridge to the southeast of Pleasant Lake, you should find it nestled against the basin headwall on the other side. Hooligan Lake is a five acre pool at 5100 feet. It is 17 feet deep and contains rainbow trout.

Hooligan Lake is not a good place to get lost. Like Pleasant Lake, it drains into the North Fork of Wooley Creek, which has no trail and hits the Wooley Creek Trail after 10 miles, 15 miles from the Wooley Creek trailhead. If you can't find your way back to Pleasant Lake, head up and over the Hooligan Lake headwall. The Bridge Creek Trail, several hundred feet down on the other side, will return you to Cuddihy Lake or Haypress Meadows. Anytime you venture off-trail in an area this remote, a compass and a good map are essential. A global positioning device would be really, really helpful.

Continuing down the Bridge Creek Trail, two miles past the Peasant Lake turnoff, you'll come to the Medicine Mountain Trail, a 2½ mile route ascending 2300 feet. After crossing Bridge Creek near some excellent campsites, the path ascends though forest and scrub to Bun's Basin. Head up Bun's Basin, briefly, to visit a couple of ponds at the base of the headwall. After that, the trail emerges onto the brushy rock face, charging to the 6837 feet summit. There's a great view of Wooley Creek, Tickner and English Peak, the Haypress Meadows area and the rest of the Wilderness (Note: There's also a brief but fantastic view of the English Peak massif from the Haypress access road).

Onemile Lake is a gem. You can get there via a half-mile, exceedingly steep trail from the saddle above Bridge Creek, or from a side trail at Ukonom Lake. To locate the latter, approaching Ukonom Lake from Johnson Hunting Ground, the path forks in the meadow just before the lake. The split is unsigned and both forks end up at Ukonom Lake. The left hand fork passes the signed turnoff to Onemile Lake.

However you go, Onemile Lake is a clear, elongated, hourglass pool surrounded by extensive and beautiful, though not especially high ridges. The lake is large at 22 acres and reasonably deep at 32 feet, with an elevation a little lower than Ukonom Lake, at 5750 feet. Brook and rainbow trout abound in this popular venue, with its brushy, densely wooded shore. The lake's southern portion is prettier, larger and much more popular than the north half. It's also where all the campsites are located.

I'm told the California fish and Game Department has inventoried more bears in the vicinity of Onemile Lake than any place else in California. People I've spoken to who have been to Onemile Lake have verified this. While I didn't see any bears, something sure upset the horses and dogs at 2:00 AM during my night at Ukonom Lake.

From a log crossing at Onemile Lake's hourglass waist, a 1½ mile path leads over the ridge to the south, to Secret Valley and Secret Lake, climbing 300 feet and dropping 800 feet. It ends up in much gentler terrain, with forest closing in. Beautiful Secret Lake covers 8½ acres at 5250 feet, in a rocky basin. It's aqua waters are 43 feet deep and contain brook and rainbow trout.

That's all I have to say about the Ukonom Lake area. Hopefully, when I go there again in 24 years, I'll find everything exactly the same.

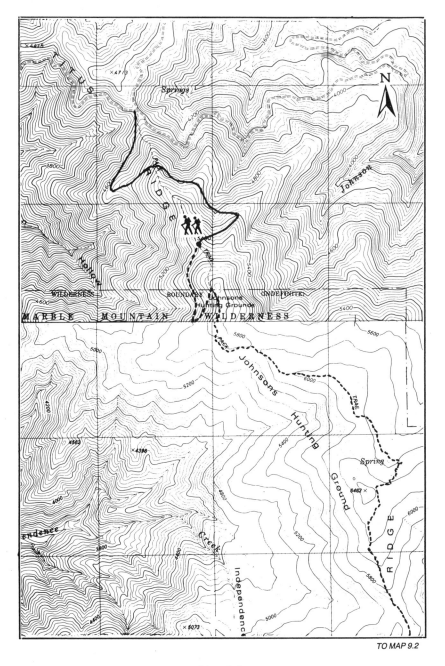

TO MAP 9.2

Map 9.1

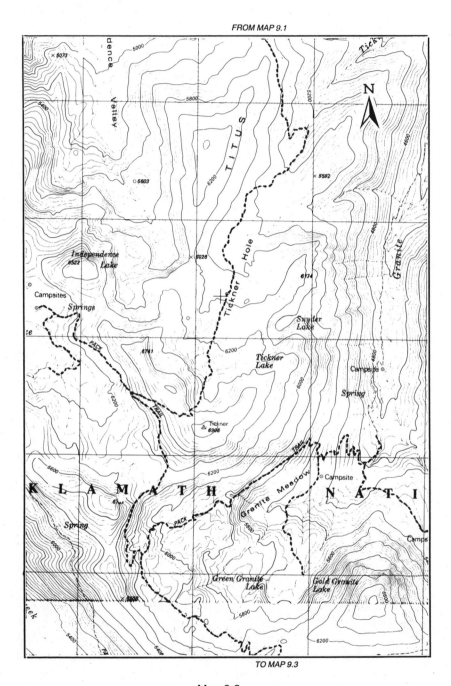

Map 9.2

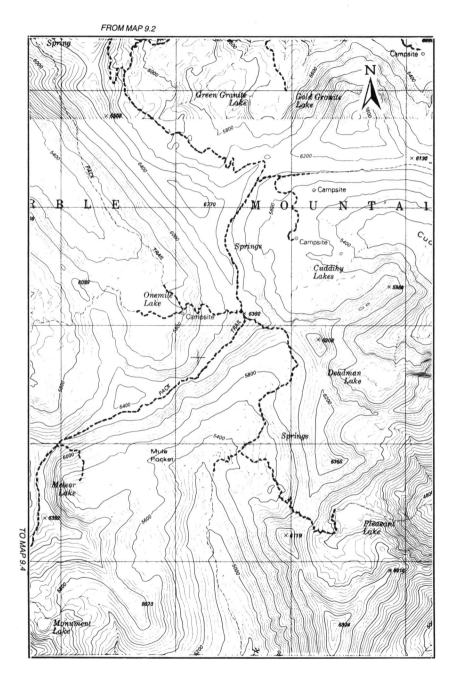

FROM MAP 9.2

Map 9.3

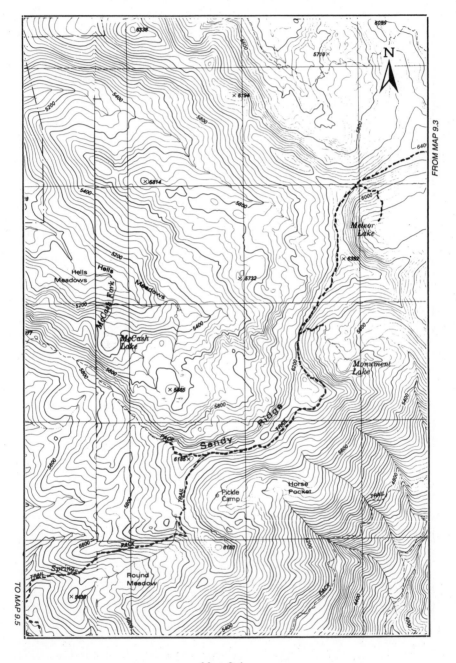

Map 9.4

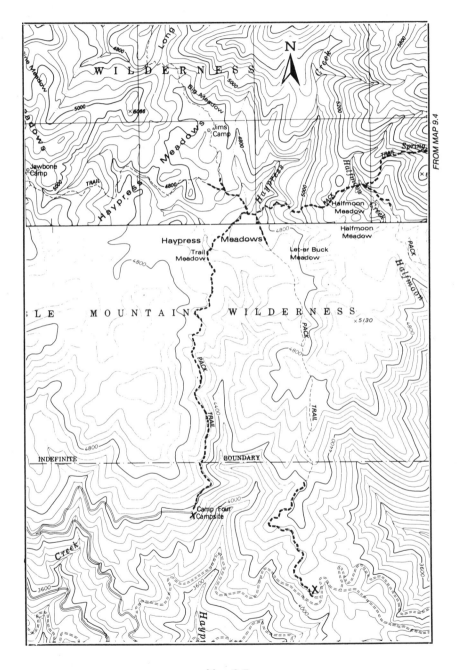

Map 9.5

10.

PACIFIC CREST TRAIL/ETNA SUMMIT TO GRIDER RIDGE

Destinations:	Marble Mountain Wilderness, Yellow Dog Mount, Shelly Lake, Shelly Meadows, Maneaten Lake, Cliff Lake, Summit Lake, Red Rock Valley, Shadow Lake, Sky High Valley, Four Corners Saddle, Little Marble Valley, Marble Valley, Box Camp Mountain, Paradise Lake, Bear Lake, Big Ridge, Buckhorn Spring, Huckleberry Mountain
Length from Etna Summit trailhead:	3 miles (S. Wilderness boundary) 11 miles (Shelly Fork Jct.) 16 miles (Kidder Lake Jct.) 24 miles (Marble Val.) 29 miles (Paradise Lake) 35 miles (Buckhorn Spring) 37½ miles (Grider trailhead)
Difficulty:	Mostly easy to Moderate.
Elevation:	5492 feet (Etna Summit trailhead) 6700 feet (S. Wilderness boundary) 6600 feet (Shelly Fork Jct.) 7300 feet (High point, above Cliff Lake) 6232 feet (Four Corners Saddle) 5900 feet (Marble Val.) 6600 feet (Box Camp Jct.) 6900 feet (Crest above Bear Lake) 6600 feet (Buckhorn Spring) 5900 feet (N. Wilderness boundary) 5200 feet (Grider trailhead)

Season:	June through October
Location:	Etna Summit - T41N-R10W-Sector 21
	Grider Ridge - T44N-R12W-Sector 5
Water:	Yes, but many long, dry stretches.
USGS 7.5" topo:	Yellow Dog Peak, Boulder Peak,
	Marble Mountain, Grider Valley.
Phone:	(916) 468-5351
Use intensity:	Moderate to light
Camping:	Idlewild (Etna Summit)
	Curly Jack (Grider Ridge)

Directions: Etna Summit. From I-5, take the Highway-3, south Yreka exit to the town of Etna. Turn right on Main Street towards Sawyer's Bar and proceed up the winding, mostly paved road to the summit. Park in the well developed parking area, which holds 30 cars. Hike north for the Marble Mountains.

Grider Ridge. Take the Highway-96 exit, 12 miles north of Yreka, and proceed on 96 to the town of Happy Camp. Turn left, in Happy Camp, onto the paved Elk Creek Road, then bear left on the narrow, blacktopped East Fork Road, which eventually becomes gravel. Signs to follow refer, variously, to Grider Ridge, Cold Springs, Huckleberry Mountain and the Pacific Crest Trail. The Grider Ridge trailhead accommodates eight cars, with just enough room to turn a trailer around.

The sign at the East Fork turnoff says, "Grider Ridge 10 miles, Cold Springs 21 miles." Actually, Cold Springs is 11 miles from the sign and five miles before the trailhead.

Where nobody ever goes: Etna Summit to Shelly Fork Junction

The original Pacific Crest Trail was supposed to follow the true Pacific Crest, up the backbone of the High Cascade range, skirting the flank of Mount Shasta and entering Oregon over the volcanic cones of Goosenest and Willow Creek Mountains. Early on, planners decided that as spectacular as the Mount Shasta route would be, a more western path, through the Trinity Alps and Marble Mountains, would be much more varied, with many more side trails and dozens of creeks and alpine lakes.

While the PCT nips a only a 16 mile corner of the vast Trinity Alps, missing its major highlights, it runs for 33 miles through the heart of the Marble Mountain Wilderness. It also neatly bisects the Russian Wilderness (see Chapter 16).

Traveling south to north on the PCT (I could just as easily have described the path north to south but that direction lost the coin toss), one begins at Etna Summit, which is a spectacular destination even if you're not hiking. See the Introduction for a description of Etna Summit. You'll find not only fantastic views of the Salmon River Canyon, Marbles and Russians, but a major trailhead development.

From Etna Summit, the path heads up a brushy ridgetop with an ever improving view of Mount Etna and the Russians to the south, and Yellow Dog Mountain to the northwest. Yellow Dog is a tremendous, barren, 7000 foot chunk of granite rising straight up from the Salmon in the Marbles' extreme southeast corner. The only trail in the vicinity is the PCT, which misses the Yellow Dog summit by two miles.

With all these panoramas to hold your interest, the path contours around the hillside, hits a saddle after a mile, then another saddle a half-mile later. After flirting with the Wilderness boundary, it enters the Wilderness for good at the headwaters of Mill Creek, one of eight Mill Creeks in Siskiyou County. A century ago, hundreds of small sawmills dotted the region and locals weren't very good at thinking up names. There are also four Fish Lakes and several Trail Creeks in the county.

A mile into the Wilderness, the path hits another saddle, at the head of Big Creek Canyon. This is quickly followed by yet another gap, over Razor Ridge into the Pointers Gulch drainage. Here the path enters a long, level, forested stretch as it contours north. Look for a huge, mossy outcropping, dripping with water, near Razor Ridge.

The next landmark, three miles up, is the crest above the Babs Fork of Kidder Creek. Soon after, things become open and rocky again as the path makes its way around the double headwaters of Glendenning Creek, then past Shotgun Creek, with its spring and small meadow, into the Shelly Lake basin.

After skirting a lateral moraine just south of Shelly Lake, the trail fords the lake's outlet creek. It's a steep, ¼ mile uphill trek to Shelly

Lake (Chapter 6). Immediately beyond the crossing lies Shelly Meadows, with the ruins of Wilson Cabin on the far end. After that, it's ¼ mile through the woods to another meadow atop a saddle, where the Shelly Fork Trail comes in on the right and departs on the left as the Bug Gulch Trail.

The two mile Shelly Fork Trail, even though it climbs 1800 feet, offers a shortcut to the heart of the PCT in the Marbles, lopping 11 of the least interesting miles, including everything just described, off the route (see Chapter 6 for directions to the Shelly Fork trailhead). North of the Shelly Fork, things get much, much better. Not that the first 11 miles were chopped liver.

The Guts: Shelly Fork to Marble Valley

Were I to recommend a single PCT segment in Northern California (above Yosemite), this would be it. The area through Mount Lassen would come next, then the stretch past Mount Eddy and Deadfall Lakes. Highlighted by the awesome beauty of the Marble Rim and the spectacular crags above Maneaten and Cliff Lakes, this portion of the PCT is incomparable.

From the Shelly Meadows junction, the path wends its level way north along the ridgetops, through forest and over rock outcroppings. Coming around a 7109 foot peak to the saddle between Haynes Fork and Timothy Gulch, the Forest Service Wilderness map shows it climbing 300 feet, crossing a crest, then dropping 500 feet, for no apparent reason. The map is wrong since the approach to the saddle is a pretty much level shot.

Beyond the saddle, the trail emerges onto bare rock as it passes tiny Fisher and Marten Lakes (Chapter 6). For the next mile, it hugs a series of rock ledges high above Kidder Creek. Look for a junction here between the PCT, heading to the right (east) above Kidder Lake, and the newer PCT Alternate, on the left, running above Maneaten Lake.

If you continue on the PCT past the Kidder Lake turnoff (Chapter 6), you'll discover why they rerouted the path to the other side of the summit (Since only Congress can re-route the PCT, the new trail is posted as an Alternate). What used to be the trail's steepest and most precarious pitch just would not hold together. And even if you made it up, the path then headed out across the north facing headwall of the Cliff Lake cirque, 1300 feet above the lake at 7100 feet. This unstable route, blasted into a nearly vertical rock face, often remains snowbound until mid-July. Getting across can be terrifying. The Alternate bypasses both the hill and the Cliff Lake headwall.

It's 1½ miles on the PCT, from the south junction with the Alternate, to Kidder Lake. Another 3½ miles on the Kidder Lake Trail takes you to the Kidder Lake trailhead.

The PCT Alternate climbs steeply to the notch above Maneaten Lake (Chapter 6). Set in an extremely steep, barren basin, Maneaten Lake rates among the deepest and most beautiful in the Wilderness. Getting down to it can be a challenge. Getting out is even worse.

After dropping briefly from the notch, the path levels off, then climbs steeply to the narrow, jagged ridge above Cliff Lake (Chapter 5). At 7200 feet, this is the highest point on the PCT in the Marbles. Lingering snow is likely on the narrow saddle above Cliff Lake, although it's not nearly as treacherous as the old route. The view is unbelievable. Cliff Lake is the second largest in the Marbles and by far the deepest at 175 feet. While there is no trail to it from the PCT, many hikers access the PCT by climbing the lake headwall.

Past Cliff Lake, the scenery settles down a little as it winds through woods and rock outcroppings far above the headwaters of Wooley Creek, the Wilderness Area's primary drainage. Look for vistas of the Wooley Creek mouth, 25 miles away and 6000 feet down. While traversing the Wooley Creek headwaters, the path hits a saddle at a gravelly flat above Summit Lake. A precarious trail leads to Summit Lake, 700 feet below and ¾ mile away. The same trail also leads to Campbell Lake in two miles and Cliff Lake in 2½ miles. Campbell Lake is the fourth largest in the Wilderness but not as scenic as Cliff Lake.

Beyond the Summit Lake saddle, the path contours around a massive, 7636 foot mountain. Although this evil looking, crown-like peak dominates the area between Cliff Lake, Red Rock Valley and Marble Valley, it has no name. Unless somebody has a better idea, I suggest Mount Bernstein.

Reentering the woods and approaching the Red Rock Canyon Trail, a close-up view of the Marble Rim appears. The Wilderness was named for this 600 to 1000 foot thick band of white marble and it constitutes the area's scenic highlight and main destination. I guarantee you won't be disappointed.

Two miles beyond the Summit Lake junction, the path hits the high pass above Red Rock Valley (Chapter 3). The Red Rock Valley Trail emerges at the Lover's Camp trailhead, 5½ miles away, after crossing a string of emerald meadows ringed in bright orange serpentine rock. A second short trail also leads north from the pass, to a small bench with a pond. A short path south from the Red Rock Valley pass, leads to Cold Springs and an excellent campsite.

The next PCT stop after Red Rock Valley, is 2½ acre Shadow Lake, ¼ mile up a side trail, on a rock ledge high above the Sky High basin (Chapter 3). The view of Sky High Lakes from Shadow Lake is outstanding. Look for a short way trail left, just beyond the Shadow Lake turnoff, to Soft Water Springs.

From Shadow Lake, it's 1½ miles along the rocky mountainside, to the upper end of the high trail to Sky High Valley. Follow it less than ¼ mile for a terrific view. Beyond the Sky High junction, the PCT drops to Four Corners Saddle (Chapter 3), ¼ mile away and 200 feet below.

At Four Corners, the two mile Marble Rim Trail and the 16 mile cross-wilderness trail to Cuddihy Lake (Chapter 9) both begin. It's a mile down the Marble Rim Trail for a mind-boggling panorama of Rainy Valley, with its 2000 foot cliffs and view of the Marble Rim's steep, west face. The Cuddihy Lake Trail's first 1½ miles drop 600 feet, then climb 400 feet to Big Elk Lake, picking up the end of the 26 mile Wooley Creek Trail on the way (Chapter 8).

The PCT is the best route through the Marble Rim area. It's a mile from Four Corners, through Little Marble Valley, to Marble Valley. In Little Marble Valley, the marble crosses the valley bottom, forming a series of glistening white clefts and fissures lush with wildflowers. A tiny crawl hole just off the trail leads to a major cave with stalactites and stalagmites. You're not likely to find it, however.

Few places in California compare to the scenery of Marble Valley. The valley's center is a grassy flat, surrounded by woods and containing a pair of small cabins. Gurgling springs flow on either side while the Marble Rim, broken in half by Marble Gap, rises directly overhead. Hang a right for the low trail to Sky High Lakes, two miles away, and the Canyon Creek Trail to Lover's Camp, 4½ miles distant.

And points north: Marble Valley to Grider Ridge

One of the Marbles' best short trails breaks off from the PCT less than ¼ mile north of Marble Valley. The Marble Gap Trail (Chapter 3), rises 900 feet in a mile to possibly the best vista in this book, a narrow, 6800 foot saddle between Rainy and Marble Valleys, with views of virtually the entire Wilderness.

The PCT segment from Marble Valley to the Box Camp Trail is described thoroughly in Chapter 3. The segment from Paradise Lake to Bear Lake is covered in Chapter 2. The intervening two miles are uneventful but pretty, affording the first views of the Red Buttes, far in the distance on the other side of the Klamath. It's four miles from Marble Valley to Paradise Lake.

On the ridge above Paradise Lake, look for a small, breadloaf shaped marble formation called Kings Castle. It used to be called Marble Mountain. So did Black Marble Mountain. At Paradise Lake, the 2½ mile Paradise Lake Trail (Chapter 2), joins the PCT, as does the seven mile South Kelsey Trail up Kelsey Creek (Chapter 1).

North of Bear Lake saddle, 1½ miles past Paradise Lake, the trail climbs a short, steep serpentinite outcropping to a 6928 foot summit, second highest on the route. Look for scattered Jeffrey pine, which grows only on serpentine in the Klamath Mountains.

The next four miles follow a mostly exposed ridgetop between the Scott River and Elk Creek. The only landmark is the junction with the Big Ridge Trail, on the right, a mile past the 6928 foot crest. It's four miles down the Big Ridge Trail to the Big Ridge trailhead. Actually, the Big Ridge Trail does not follow Big Ridge, it leads to it. The PCT follows Big Ridge.

Look for views down Grider Valley as you approach Buckhorn Mountain, with the Red Buttes rising on the other side of the Klamath. Were you to remain on the PCT, you'd hit the Red Buttes in two to three days. You can save 22 fairly boring miles by skipping Grider Creek and rejoining the PCT in Seiad Valley. The hike from Seiad Valley to the Red Buttes, via the Devil's Peaks, is outstanding. See "Best Day-Hikes of the California Northwest," (Mountain N'Air Books, 1991)

At Buckhorn Mountain, the path crosses a last band of marble, then passes Buckhorn Spring, 2½ miles from the north trailhead. Beyond the campsite at Buckhorn Spring, the route begins a 1200 foot descent to the 5400 foot trailhead, entering the woods a final time a mile beyond the spring. Where it enters the woods, a side trail takes off to the 6300 foot summit of Huckleberry Mountain, a densely forested, not very interesting peak. Soon after, the PCT leaves the Wilderness and drops steeply down to the Grider Ridge trailhead.

After leaving the Marbles, reaching Oregon via the PCT requires crossing the Klamath River and would even if they'd used the Mount Shasta route. At the town of Seiad Valley, just north of the Marbles, the Klamath's elevation lies at 1700 feet. At Copco Lake, north of Shasta, the Klamath is only slightly higher at 2100 feet. Although only 300 miles long, the Klamath ranks as one of only three rivers to breach the Sierra-Cascade mountain chain. The others are the Columbia and the Sacramento.

A mile or so down the Elk Creek/Grider Ridge Road from the trailhead, the road crosses one last marble outcropping. Just thought I'd let you know

Taylor Lake

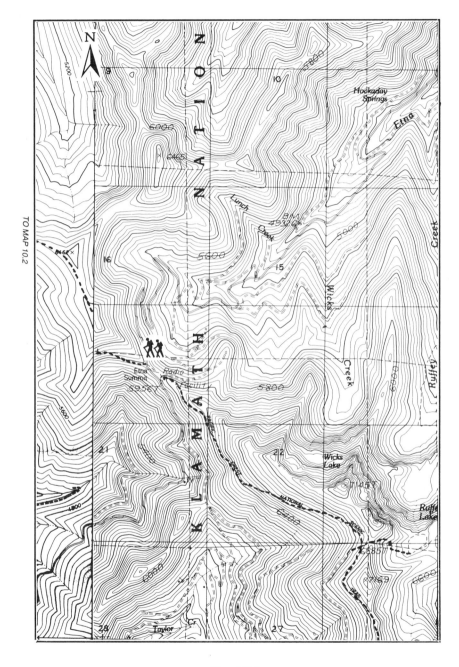

Map 10.1

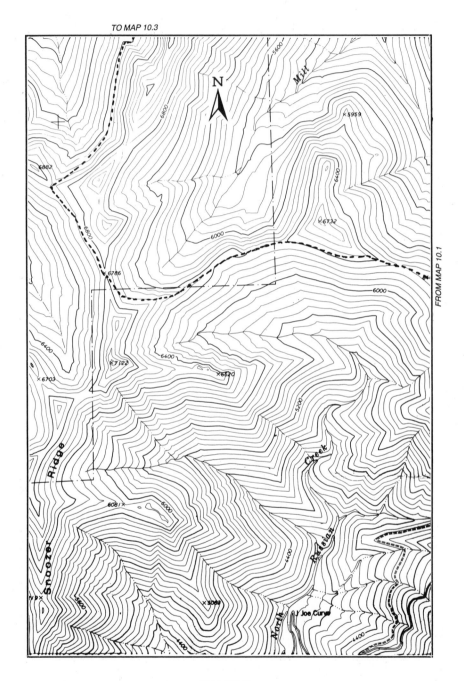

Map 10.2

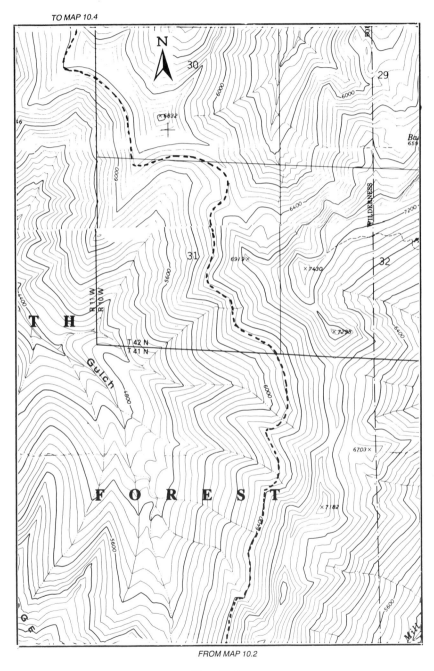

Map 10.3

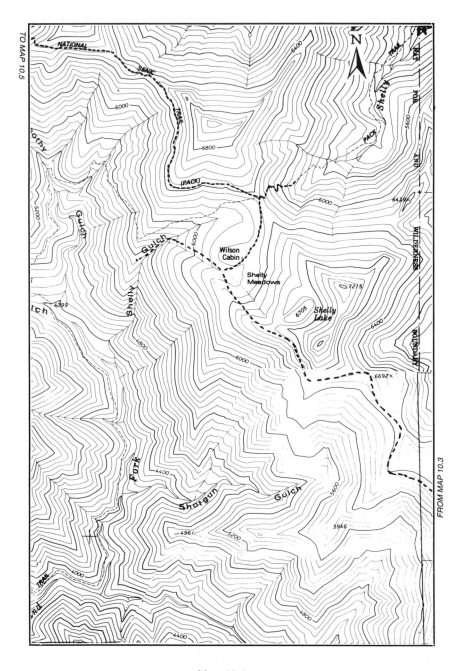

Map 10.4

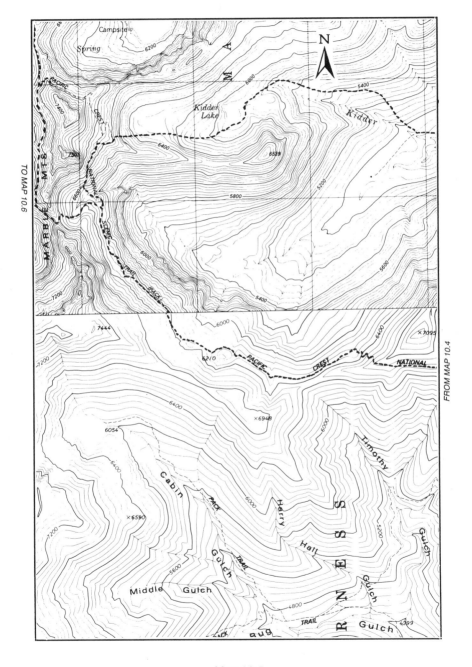

Map 10.5

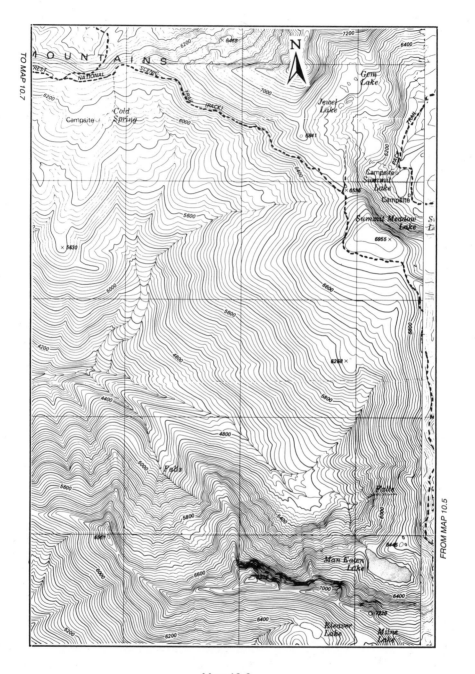

Map 10.6

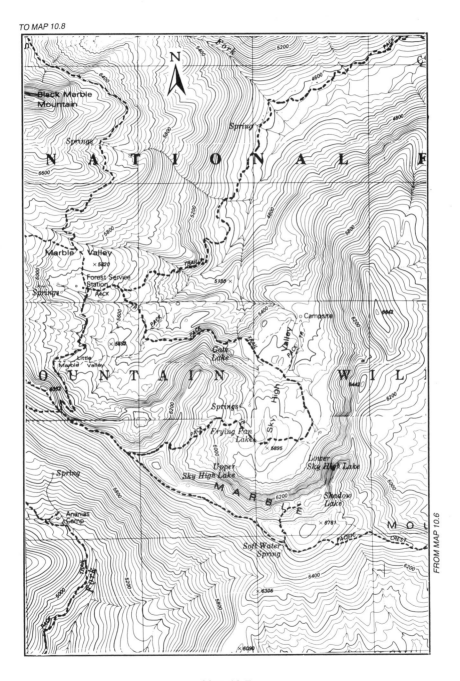

Map 10.7

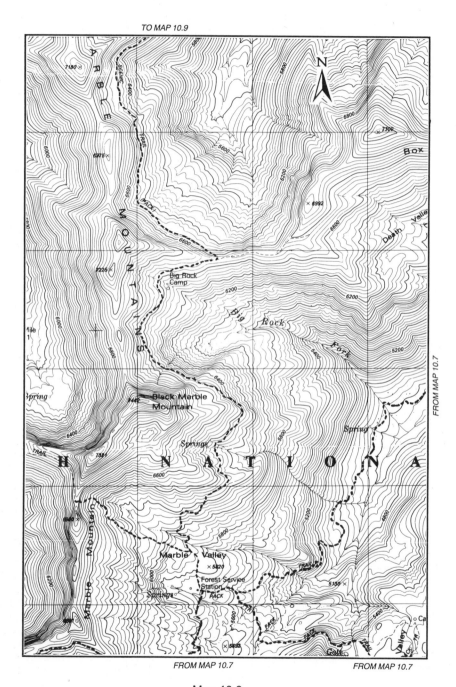

TO MAP 10.9

FROM MAP 10.7

FROM MAP 10.7

FROM MAP 10.7

Map 10.8

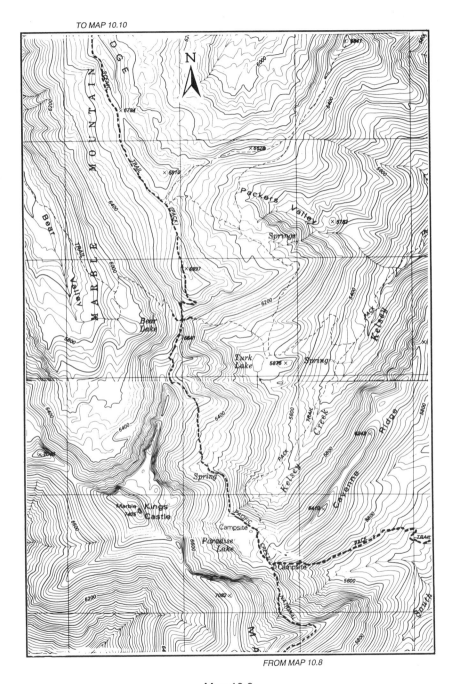

Map 10.9

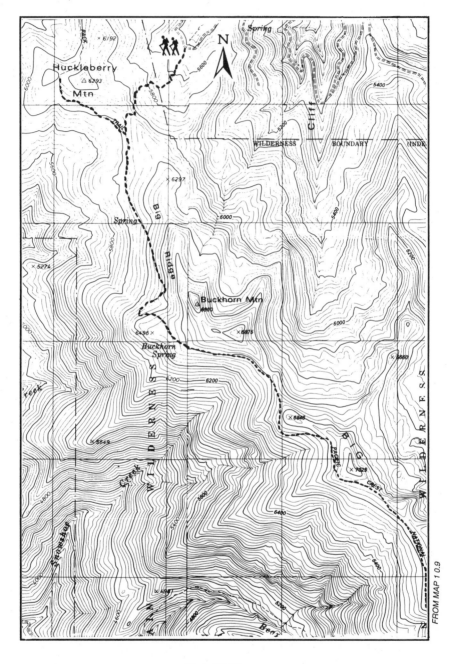

Map 10.10

THE RUSSIAN WILDERNESS AREA

Rugged Landscape, typical of Russian Wilderness Area.
Cliff above South Sugar Lake.

11.   TAYLOR/HOGAN/BIG BLUE LAKES

Destinations:	Taylor Lake, Twin Lakes, Hogan Lake, Big Blue Lake.
Length:	½ mile (Taylor)
	3 (to 4) miles (Hogan)
	3½ miles (Big Blue)
Water:	All over the place
Season:	June through October
Difficulty:	Easy (Taylor)
	Difficult (Hogan)
	Yikes! (Big Blue)
	Elevation:
	6200 feet to 6500 feet (Taylor)
	5900 feet (Hogan)
	6800 (Big Blue)
USGS 7.5" topo:	Russian Peak
Location:	T41N-R10W-Sector 27
Use intensity	Heavy (Taylor)
	Light (Hogan)
Camping:	Idlewild CG
Phone:	(916) 467-5757

Directions: From I-5, take the south Yreka exit and follow Highway-3 to Etna. Turn right on Main Street and follow the mostly paved road to Etna Summit. Take the first dirt road left, a half-mile past the summit, and follow signs to the roomy Taylor Lake trailhead. The road is very steep in spots but wide and not too bumpy.

Taylor Lake: Everyman's wilderness

Taylor Lake may be the most accessible high mountain lake located inside a Wilderness Area, in all Northern California. The half-mile trail is nearly level and built to accommodate wheelchairs. It's a great place to take in-laws from back East who aren't into hiking but want a feel for the area's back country.

Even without the hike, the ride to the trailhead is breathtaking. Stop at Etna Summit for a panorama of the North Fork of the Salmon River, flanked by the Marble Mountains to the north and the Russian Mountains to the south. Barren, towering granite peaks jut up everywhere as you approach the trailhead on the dirt access road.

The elongated, half-mile long lake, occupies a handsome glacial cirque, with white cliffs rising on three sides and forests of red fir, white pine and mountain hemlock lining most of the shore. At the lake's upper end, a marshy corn lily meadow, with masses of willow brush, guards the base of the main headwall.

The popular lake covers 12 acres at 6500 feet elevation, although it looks much larger. The lake is 35 feet deep and stocked with brook trout. Many outstanding campsites line its banks.

If you continue driving up the road from the trailhead, it ends at the Pacific Crest Trail in ¾ mile (Chapter 16). It's a 1½ mile walk to the same road end from the PCT crossing at Etna Summit. Both trailheads offer easy access to Ruffey Lake, Meeks Meadow Lake and Smith Lake, all small, shallow, very pretty and outside the Wilderness Area.

Hogan and Big Blue Lakes: Not quite so easy

My mistake, the day I visited Hogan Lake, was not studying the map carefully enough. It appeared an easy, two mile trek from Taylor Lake, the exact distance stated on the sign where the trail exits the Taylor Lake basin. Had I taken the time to calculate the elevation changes, it would prepared me for the fact that to reach Hogan Lake, the trail rises 400 feet in a half-mile, then drops 1000 feet in a mile, before leveling off the last half-mile.

Actually, I dispute all distances except the 1000 feet in a mile. It took me 1½ hours to reach Hogan Lake from Taylor Lake and two hours to get back. By my gut reckoning and usual hiking pace, that's around three miles.

From Taylor Lake, the path climbs a series of meadows, then some rock outcroppings, before leveling off in a pole stand of young conifers. Soon after, it makes a significant but brief drop before rising to a rocky crest.

Beyond the crest, the path drops and drops and drops and drops. Being unprepared, I panicked and almost turned back. The plunge is mostly forested, although the trees are well spaced with much grass in-between.

Eventually, the trail bottoms out at Hogan Creek, which it follows for a rocky, faint in places, mostly shaded mile to the lake, bisecting a couple meadows on the way.

Although not as pretty as Taylor Lake, I liked Hogan Lake. After the dizzying descent to get there, however, and the steep walls soaring from the shore on three sides, I felt like I'd fallen into an oubliette (a Medieval dungeon which opens only in the ceiling). It is not a place for the claustrophobic.

Campsites are confined to the rectangular lake's wooded north bank, around the outlet, where the trail comes in. Much smaller than Taylor Lake at 7½ acres, the 5900 foot elevation lake reaches a depth of 26 feet. Fishing for rainbow and brook trout is supposed to be excellent.

Hogan Lake's most impressive feature is the series of white rock cliffs rising to the southeast. It's comforting to know that a half-mile away, and 800 feet up the cliffs, lies Big Blue Lake. Big Blue is twice the size of Taylor Lake, three times larger than Hogan Lake, four times prettier than either...and has no trail access.

If you follow the Hogan Lake shore to the left (south), from the trail end to the first inlet creek, then make your way up the creek, you should find a very faint way trail to Big blue Lake. I chickened out when the path took off up an exposed rock slope with a nearly 100% grade, which appeared to go on forever. I'd have given it a shot were my wife not waiting back at Taylor Lake and if I didn't have that 1000 foot hill to worry about on the return trip. To reach Big Blue

Lake from Hogan Lake, they tell me to just keep following the stream, and/or the valley bottom, up the hill. What valley bottom?

There are better routes to Big Blue Lake. Probably the best is via Albers Lake (Chapter 12. "Albert Lake" on some maps). Hike up the head of the basin to the ridge, which isn't too difficult, and you'll find Big Blue Lake far below, on the other side. Getting down the cliffs and loose talus to the lake is another matter. To me, Big Blue Lake belongs more to the Taylor-Hogan cluster and than the Paynes-Albers cluster.

If you're a little gutsy or happen to have a global positioning device on you, try contouring around to the left from the rocky crest between Taylor and Hogan Lakes, just before the path starts downhill. With luck, you may locate a way trail. If not, simply hold your contour until you reach Twin Lakes, in a half-mile. The twins each cover less than an acre in a small, wooded cirque at 6300 feet. The shallow ponds contain brook trout.

From Twin Lakes, continue your contour around the hillside to the south, above Hogan Lake, until you reach the Big Blue outlet, then follow the creek ¼ mile uphill to the lake. This is not an easy route, with much brush and loose talus.

Big Blue is a magnificent, crescent shaped aqua pool in the bottom of a white, steep walled, almost totally enclosed, treeless cirque which often retains snow well into July. It's one of the region's most beautiful lakes. Fairly large at 17 acres, the deep basin plunges 96 feet below the water line. At an elevation of 6800 feet, the lake is home to rainbow and brown trout. The only decent campsite lies near the outlet.

Pat Bernstein chills out at Taylor Lake

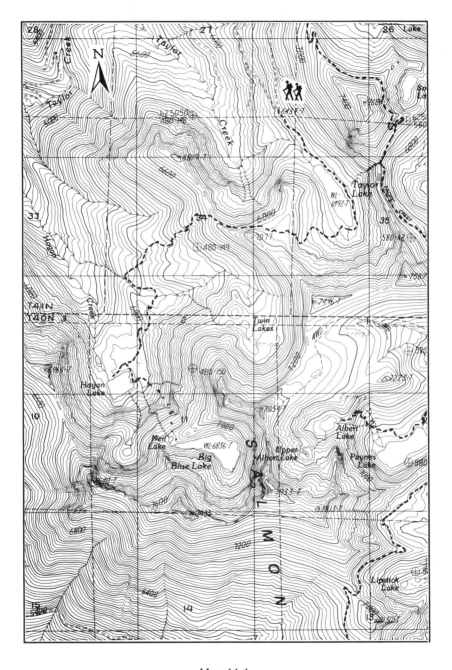

Map 11.1

12.   PAYNES LAKE

Destinations:	Paynes Lake, Lower Albers Lake, Upper Albers Lake, Pacific Crest Trail
Length:	3 miles
Water:	At lake
Season:	June through October
Difficulty:	Difficult
Elevation:	4400 to 6500 feet (Paynes) 6900 feet (Lower Albers)
USGS 7.5" topo:	Russian Peak
Location:	T40N-R9W-Sector 6
Use intensity:	Moderate
Camping:	Indian Scotty
Phone:	(916) 468-5351

Directions: Leave I-5 at the south Yreka (Highway-3) exit. Follow Highway-3 past Etna to French Creek Road. Proceed to the end of the road, noting where it joins Sugar Creek Road so you won't get lost on the way back (although both roads end up on Highway-3). Turn right at the "T" junction with the sign pointing to Paynes Lake. Follow the narrow, rather rough dirt road to the roomy, well marked trailhead.

A Payne to get to

The prettiest of northern California's alpine glacial lakes all lie within areas of white granite. Unlike other rock types, granite tends to erode into rounded domes and has a soft-edged beauty all its own. It's the reason for the great popularity of the Trinity Alps and Sierra Nevada. One of Northern California's loveliest granite-set glacial lakes is Paynes Lake.

The surrounding Russian Mountains are noted for their botanical diversity as well as their beauty. This is described in detail in Chapters 13 and 14. Look for Brewer spruce, red fir, white fir, Western white pine, mountain hemlock, lodgepole pine, Sadler oak, rhododendron, evergreen chinkapin and scrub tanoak. Like I said, it's diverse.

The trail follows a thinly soiled, sparsely wooded granite ridge between two deep valleys. The first 1½ miles of steep switchbacks, logged in the lower portions, seems interminable. You know you're halfway there when you come to an all-too-brief level spot in a little shaded cove. The path then steepens again, and becomes more open as it approaches the Paynes Lake cirque.

Paynes Lake covers 16½ acres and is 50 feet deep. At an elevation of 6500 feet, it is home to brook and rainbow trout. There are numerous campsites near the outlet and along the north shore.

While Duck Lake (Chapter 13), is larger and possibly prettier, it looks smaller because the basin around Paynes Lake is wider. Much level, gently shaded, not too brushy land surrounds the lake. Sparkling white granite domes thrust up on two sides and a vast meadow adorns the hillside immediately north of the main rock headwall.

The Pacific Crest Trail crosses the Paynes Lake Trail just below the lake. For the energetic, it's six miles north on the PCT to Etna Summit. Head south and it's six miles to Bingham Lake, along the stark, west wall of Russian Peak.

The Paynes Lake Trail continues past the lake, shooting steeply up the meadow and nearby rock faces, to Lower and Upper Albers Lakes, called "Albert Lakes" on some maps. It's only a half-mile to the tiny, exquisite pools stocked with brook and rainbow trout. The lower lake covers 2½ acres at 6900 feet and is 15 feet deep. The upper lake, ⅛ mile up the inlet stream to the southwest, covers two acres at 7100 feet and is also 15 feet deep.

If you head uphill to the west from Lower Albers Lake, to an obvious saddle, ⅓ mile away and 500 feet overhead, you'll come out above gorgeous Big Blue Lake, one of the region's largest (17 acres) and most difficult to reach. Getting down to the lake from the saddle is far more difficult than hiking to the saddle from Lower Albers Lake. Other routes to Big Blue Lake, none of them easy, are described in Chapter 11.

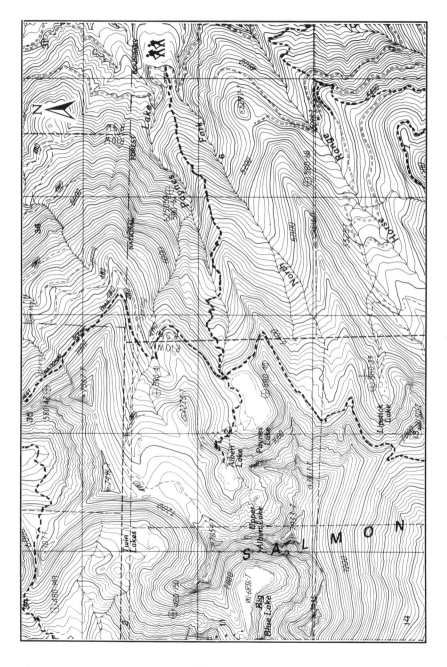

Map 12.1

13. DUCK/EATON/HORSESHOE LAKES

Destinations:	Big Duck Lake, Little Duck Lake, Eaton Lakes, Horseshoe Lake, Lipstick Lake, Josephine Lake, Horse Range Lakes, Duck Lake Special Interest Area.
Length:	4½ miles (Big Duck, Eaton, Horseshoe)
Water:	OK
Season:	June through October
Difficulty:	Moderate
Elevation:	4800 to 6400 (Big Duck), 6600 feet (Eaton) 6700 feet (Little Duck)
USGS 7.5" topo:	Russian Peak
Location:	T40N-R9W-Sector 6
Use:	Non-motorized only
Use intensity:	Moderate
Camping:	Indian Scotty
Phone:	(916) 468-5351

Directions: From Highway 3, between Etna and Callahan, take French Creek Road (which eventually merges with Sugar Creek Road), to the junction where a sign points right to Duck and Paynes Lakes. Turn right and continue 1.3 miles, past the bridge over Duck Lake Creek, to a short turnout on the left. The former logging landing holds 30 cars.

❖ ❖ ❖

Duck, a lake!

In 1970, the Russian Mountains were little known and seldom visited, except by local fishermen. Back then, there were few trailhead markings. I located the Duck Lake Trail by driving a maze of logging roads, parking at a washout at Duck Lake Creek, and beating the bushes up and down the road. Many of these roads are now closed off and inside the Wilderness. And while I love hiking, I also enjoy driving and sightseeing. I find it the height of frustration to have to hike a perfectly driveable road.

Even with the closed roads, it's not that far to the high lakes accessible from the Duck Lake trailhead. They're certainly worth a peek in this exquisite mountain paradise. So, as the saying goes, may the trail rise up to meet you.

Before describing these pathways, I should discuss the musical trailheads on the east side of the Marbles and Russians. If you've been to Duck Lake before, be advised that the current trailhead is nowhere near the old one. The old one accessed a route which itself was $1\frac{1}{2}$ miles longer than the path from the original, pre-wilderness trailhead. The problem is that most roads abutting the east side of the Russian and Marble Mountain Wilderness Areas are on private timberland and maintained by the landowner. Some of these lands and roads lie inside the Wilderness. When the private owner recently reopened a road they owned which cut across a corner of the Wilderness, to haul logs from a logging operation not in the Wilderness, the Forest Service requested they find an alternate route. The owner ultimately agreed to relinquish all rights to the road in exchange for no longer maintaining the final, one mile spur to the Duck Lake trailhead.

The trailhead was moved 500 feet downhill, to a new location on a different road. The down side is that new trail is $1\frac{1}{2}$ miles longer than the old one and three miles longer than the original route. The up side is that visitation at Duck lake has been reduced by 80%.

To reach Duck, Eaton and Horseshoe Lakes, follow the path up from the new trailhead. It climbs a logging road for a short ways, then becomes trail. The new route switches steeply back and forth on the ridge between Duck Lake Creek and Horse Range Creek. Finally, it emerges onto a road ($\frac{1}{4}$ mile from the old trailhead), cuts across a switchback, then comes out on the same road again. Go right, along the road, here, for Lipstick, Horse Range and Josephine Lakes.

For Duck and Eaton Lakes, follow the road/trail steeply uphill, through the woods, before emerging onto a high road. Turn left on the high road, following the signs. After a level half-mile, the original, upper trailhead is finally reached.

The upper trailhead is actually two trailheads 100 feet apart. The Eaton Lake Trail comes first, then the Duck Lake Trail. If you continue up the closed road, instead of taking one of the trails, you'll end up at Horseshoe Lake in 1½ miles.

Above the upper trailhead, the Duck Lake Trail contains a few steep pitches, especially near the beginning. It isn't nearly as bad as the Paynes or Eaton Lake Trails, however. The path climbs through woods of red fir, western white pine, mountain hemlock and Brewer spruce, with lodgepole pine at the lake. A one mile side route to Little Duck Lake breaks off a half-mile below Duck Lake.

The last pitch to Big Duck Lake winds through a maze of giant white boulders, remarkable for their smooth roundness. It's a lovely area. The surrounding peaks aren't as impressive as at Paynes Lake (Chapter 12), but the gentle granite domes and white rock shore are exquisite. The woods are denser than at Paynes Lake and the banks steeper.

At 26 acres, Big Duck is the largest lake in the Russian Wilderness, although the surrounding basin is smaller than that of Paynes Lake, the second largest. Big Duck Lake is 27 feet deep, at 6400 feet elevation, and stocked with brook and rainbow trout.

From the turnoff below Big Duck Lake, it's one mile, and a 700 foot rise, to Little Duck Lake, nesting 300 feet higher than its larger cousin. The Little Duck basin is a tad roomier than Big Duck's, with much more exposed rock, although the cliffs aren't as steep. Little Duck Lake covers five acres, reaches a depth of 18 feet and is stocked with brook trout.

The Duck Lake drainage has been designated a Special Interest Area/Botanical Area, to highlight the botanical diversity for which Russian Peak is famous. Of the famous "17 conifer species" found within the Russian Wilderness, most can be seen in the Duck Lake area, although not always alongside the trail. The 17 species include 14 fairly common to the region, plus three "glacial relics," or isolated populations whose main range lies way to the north or south.

One such species, foxtail pine, can be found on the ridge directly south of Little Duck Lake. This is its only known occurrence in the Russian Wilderness. It turns up in a few places in the Marbles and Trinity Alps, then isn't seen again until the upper reaches of the east slope of the high Sierra, 800 miles south.

Virtually the only California populations of Englemann spruce, subalpine fir and Pacific silver fir, are located in the vicinity of Duck Lake. See Chapter 14 for more on botanical diversity in the Russian Wilderness, and a list of the 17 species.

It would be fun to report that I observed big ducks at Big Duck Lake and little ducks at Little Duck Lake. I noted no ducks at either, however.

Eaton Lake: Horseshoe lipstick

The two Eaton Lakes grace the end of the well marked trail near the upper Duck Lake trailhead. The path borders on monstrous, rising 1000 feet in the final ¾ mile. The route is faint in places and rather rocky. Or, put another way, the route will make you faint in places and you're off your rocker if...

Never mind.

Eaton Lake occupies 13 acres in a tight, wooded cirque on the flank of Eaton Peak, second highest in the Wilderness at 7600 feet and one of the more prominent summits visible from Scott Valley. The lake is 27 feet deep and stocked with rainbow trout. Upper Eaton Lake is a small pond immediately above Eaton Lake.

To reach Horseshoe Lake, continue up the closed road from the upper trailheads, instead of taking the Eaton or Duck Lake Trails. It's a little over a mile to the lake, with a rise of 800 feet. The fact that it's a road, not a trail, makes the going much easier, with a couple of level stretches breaking the monotony. The lake covers six acres in a wooded cirque. It is 21 feet deep and stocked with rainbow trout.

My biggest problem with Horseshoe Lake is that even though a perfectly nice road leads all the way there, you can't drive to it. My second biggest problem is that it's not shaped like a horseshoe, although it is mildly kidney shaped. Perhaps somebody once found (or lost) a horseshoe there.

Should you make your way up the head of the Horseshoe Lake basin for ¾ mile, above the lake, off the trail and up the cliffs; you might succeed in locating Josephine Lake, a shallow two acre pond supposedly chock full of brook trout. Josephine Lake is 1000 feet higher than Horseshoe Lake (7400 versus 6400 feet), making it the highest lake in the Wilderness. It is definitely not an easy hike.

Where the route from the main, lower trailhead first hits a closed road, cuts across the switchback, then hits the same road again, head right instead of left for the Lipstick Lake Trail. You'll see a sign, eventually. If you continue on the path towards Duck Lake, to the next road crossing up, then go right instead of left, you'll still end up at Lipstick Lake.

I don't know why they call it Lipstick Lake. Perhaps somebody found (or lost) a horseshoe there.

It's four miles to Lipstick Lake from the lower trailhead, with a rise of 2000 feet. Eventually, the road turns into a trail. The 1½ acre pond, set in a little rocky basin at 6400 feet elevation, is only nine feet deep but contains brook trout.

To reach the Horse Range Lakes, watch for the crossing of Horse Range Creek on the Lipstick Lake route. It's a brushy, 2½ mile, off-trail journey, rising 1200 feet to an elevation of 6600 feet, to the three tiny ponds at the head of a large meadowed basin with rocky cliffs overhead. The largest pond covers two acres, with a depth plummeting a whopping five feet. There are no Loch Ness monsters here, only a few brook trout.

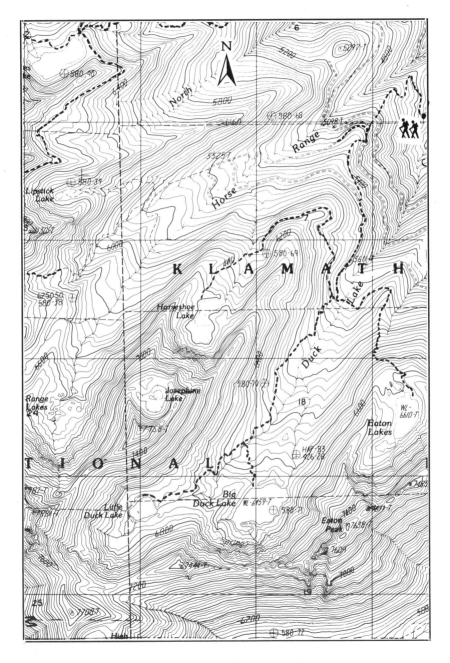

Map 13.1

14. BINGHAM LAKE/SUGAR LAKES

Destinations:	Bingham Lake, Jackson Lake, Sugar Lake, S. Sugar Lake, High Lake.
Length:	½ mile (Bingham)
	3 miles (Sugar)
Difficulty:	Moderate
Elevation:	300 feet (trailhead)
	7500 feet (Ridge above Bingham)
	7000 feet (Bingham)
	6900 feet (S. Sugar)
	5900 feet (Sugar)
	7300 feet (High)
Season:	June through October
Water:	Lots in lakes
USGS 7.5" topo:	Russian Peak
Location:	T40N-R9W-Sector 31 (Bingham)
Use intensity:	Light
Camping:	Trail Creek
Phone:	(916) 467-5757

Directions: *Bingham Lake.* Take I-5 to the south Yreka exit and follow Highway-3 to Callahan. At Callahan, turn right onto the paved South Fork Salmon Road, towards Cecilville. The Bingham Lake turnoff is unsigned, eight miles up. Look for a wide gravel road emerging onto the pavement, in a stand of large incense cedar. If you miss it, proceed to the summit, then double back three miles. It will be the second side road on the left, a mile after a tight switchback. For the record, the sideroad is called 41N16.

From the unmarked turnoff, follow the wide, sometimes a little bumpy, dirt and gravel road to a switchback at a locked gate. Continue on the main road, past the gate and around the switchback, to a major intersection where the first sign ("Bingham Lake Trail") appears. Make a hard left, up the hill, for *Bingham Lake*. While the beautiful, well signed, well groomed trailhead holds 10 cars, turnaround room may be a little tight for trailers. There's a huge parking area a mile before the trailhead.

Sugar Lake. If you continue straight instead of making a hard right at the intersection with the Bingham Lake sign, you'll come out on road 41N14. Turn left on 41N14 for the Sugar Creek Trail, three miles up. You can also reach 41N14 from the Cecilville-Callahan Road. The turnoff is marked "Sugar Lake, Duck Lake, Paynes Lake." Park at the turnout just over the Sugar Creek bridge (the only bridge until Duck Lake Creek), on the north (far) side of the creek. There is no trailhead sign and the start of the trail has been obliterated. From the parking area, hike up the boulders beginning near a large, rotted, upright tree trunk. Climb through the small notch, then follow the path of least resistance until you pick up the faint trail.

Bingham Lake: A major misadventure

While becoming totally disoriented in my off-trail hike around Bingham Lake seemed hilarious afterwards, I sure wasn't laughing at the time. Here's what happened:

I found the trailhead easily enough. It's difficult to miss. They've recently pushed the access road even closer to the lake and it's now the highest trailhead in the region, at 7300 feet (although to keep things in perspective, 7300 feet is the elevation of downtown Mexico City). This is also one of the prettiest trailheads, amid granite cliffs in the subalpine forest zone, directly above Jackson Lake and within view of Thompson Peak, highest point in the Trinity Alps, and Callahan Summit.

As the house and outbuildings confirm, Jackson Lake lies outside the Russian Wilderness. The 28 acre pool, at 6200 feet elevation, is 77 feet deep and probably crammed to the gills with fish. It is also privately owned and not stocked by the Fish and Game Department. I was strongly advised against trespassing. Not that I would.

From the trailhead, the Bingham Lake route follows the final, closed off ⅛ mile of the road, with several brand new signs directing you to the trail. When you finally arrive at the highly touted pedal pathway, it disappears after 20 feet. Honest.

No matter, simply head uphill. You may or may not pick up the trail again but it's less than ¼ mile to the knife-edge ridgetop above Bingham Lake. A faint way trail leads from the ridge down to this truly magnificent pool, set in a tight basin surrounded by nearly vertical white cliffs.

The best way to reach the lake, it seemed to me, was to hike down the ridge to the left, which quickly drops to the outlet and is better defined than the so-called trail. Russian Peak, high point of the Wilderness at 8196 feet, towers above the outlet's opposite shore.

The only spot level enough to stand on in the Bingham Lake basin, let alone camp, occurs at the tree-clogged outlet. This is no place for horses. The lake covers 8½ acres at 7050 feet and is 55 feet deep. It is supposedly stocked with brook and rainbow trout, although if they stock by aerial drop, I can't imagine how they'd get a plane near the lake.

Dipping a toe in Bingham Lake wasn't on my agenda the day I visited, only taking a picture from above. After photographing the lake, I planned to hike along the ridgetop, off-trail, until I could see South Sugar Lake. Depending on the lay of the land, I also considered climbing Russian Peak, rising from the ridge between Bingham and South Sugar.

Where I first hit the ridge above Bingham Lake, I found the lake view obscured. Seeking a better vantage point, I hiked up the crest a short way, towards South Sugar Lake (right/east). After a couple hundred yards, I left the ridge for five minutes, making my way around a small outcropping. Immediately after, at the ridge again, I was rewarded with an outstanding panorama of the lake, Russian Peak, Scott Valley, etc.

After that, I struggled to make it around to the spot on the ridge where Russian Peak took off. But the farther I went, the rockier and brushier things became. At the end, I was climbing over giant boulders and making virtually no progress. So much for South Sugar Lake and Russian Peak, I thought.

It wasn't until I got home and studied the map more carefully, that I became totally confused. For one thing, there should have been a 7800 foot high intersecting ridge on the right (east), between the Bingham and South Sugar basins. I saw no such ridge and couldn't imagine failing to notice such a landmark. Also, Bingham Lake drains into the Salmon River, not Scott Valley.

I finally figured out that when I left the ridge above Bingham Lake for five minutes, for a better vantage point, I was above South Sugar Lake when I returned, not Bingham Lake. The two basins appear remarkably similar and I hadn't gotten that good an initial look at Bingham Lake. The ridge I attempted to hike, towards what I took to be Russian Peak, was actually the intersecting ridge, forming the south wall of South Sugar Lake basin. The intersecting ridge's high point is Grizzly Peak, an impressive, narrow spire which struck me as impossible to scale without climbing gear.

In retrospect, my plan to climb Russian Peak by hiking around the Bingham Lake ridgetop, would not have worked. The saddle between the two basins is topped by a row of giant, upward pointing stone knives, with sheer cliffs on either side and no place to walk. The most popular Russian Peak climbing route begins at the far side of the Bingham Lake outlet. It's 500 feet lower than the ridge and very steep and rocky, but do-able.

The South Sugar Lake basin is slightly wider and more open than that of Bingham Lake, albeit no less beautiful. I passed a sort of way trail to the lake, but it didn't look very promising. If hiking by dead reckoning makes you uncomfortable, try the Sugar Lake Trail, described shortly. South Sugar Lake covers 3½ acres at 6850 feet and is stocked with rainbow trout.

To return to the trailhead, I retraced the route along the ridgetop but could not find the site where I first saw Bingham Lake. Instead, I picked a likely spot and headed downhill, praying that I would come out before, not after the road end. If I'd miscalculated, I would be in for a mighty long walk. As it turned out, I emerged exactly at the trailhead. For some reason, that's how things usually turn out when I get lost.

A Sugar High

There are better ways to reach Sugar and South Sugar Lakes than the ridgetop above Bingham Lake. One is the Sugar Lake Trail. Because of the preservation objective in the Sugar Creek drainage, recreation is being de-emphasized and the trail is unmaintained and unmarked. It is not that difficult to find or follow, however.

It's three miles through the deep woods to Sugar Lake, with a rise from 4800 to 5900 feet. The lake covers 2½ acres and is six feet deep, in a beautiful, white rock basin. Its green water contains a naturally reproducing rainbow trout population.

Halfway up the path, South Sugar Creek comes in on the left. Follow the creek and/or way trail to South Sugar Lake, 1½ miles away and 1000 feet higher than Sugar Lake, in a more open basin. See the previous section for details.

The Sugar Creek drainage is among the most botanically diverse in a Wilderness famous for botanical diversity. It is exceeded only by Duck Lake Creek (Chapter 13) and South Russian Creek (Chapter 15) and is a prime Englemann spruce area. Watch for this species as you hike. The species' only California incursion includes a small population near Burney Falls, and extensive stands in the Russian Peak area. Its main range pretty much ends at Crater Lake, 150 miles north.

Of the Russian Wilderness Area's famous "17 conifer species," nearly all turn up in the Sugar Creek drainage, although not always alongside the trail. The 17 species include 14 common to the region (Douglas-fir, ponderosa pine, sugar pine, white fir, incense cedar, Western white pine, lodgepole pine, whitebark pine, knobcone pine, mountain hemlock, Shasta red fir, Brewer spruce, common juniper and Pacific yew), plus three "glacial relics," or isolated populations whose main range lies far to the north or south (foxtail pine, Engelmann spruce and subalpine fir).

Actually, two lists I've seen differ. The above is taken from a Forest Service flyer, with a slight correction. The flyer lists "mountain hemlock" (Tsuga heterophylla) as "Western hemlock" (Tsuga mertensiana), which must be a mistake. I've never seen Western hemlock anywhere near Siskiyou County while mountain hemlock is quite common. Another list, in the Forest Botanist's office, substitutes Pacific silver fir for knobcone pine. So there may be 18 species. I wouldn't be surprised to find a Jeffrey pine or two, either. In the whole of the Marbles and Russians, there are 25 known conifer species. See Chapter 14 for more on botanical diversity in the Russian Wilderness.

Grizzley Peak above South Sugar Lake

Compare this to Mount Shasta, where elevations in the 7000 foot range are home only to mountain hemlock and Shasta red fir. Recent glaciation and/or volcanic activity may have had something to do with that.

The best route to the isolated and lovely High Lake begins at Sugar Lake. Follow the inlet creek northwest to the ridge between Sugar and Little Duck Lakes, then contour south for $\frac{1}{8}$ mile. The elevation of the $3\frac{1}{2}$ acre lake is 7300 feet, making it the second highest in the Russian Wilderness after Josephine Lake (Chapter 13). The lake contains brook and rainbow trout.

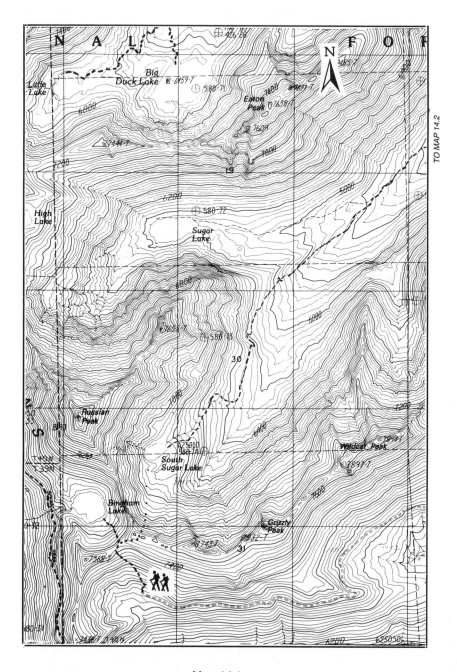

Map 14.1

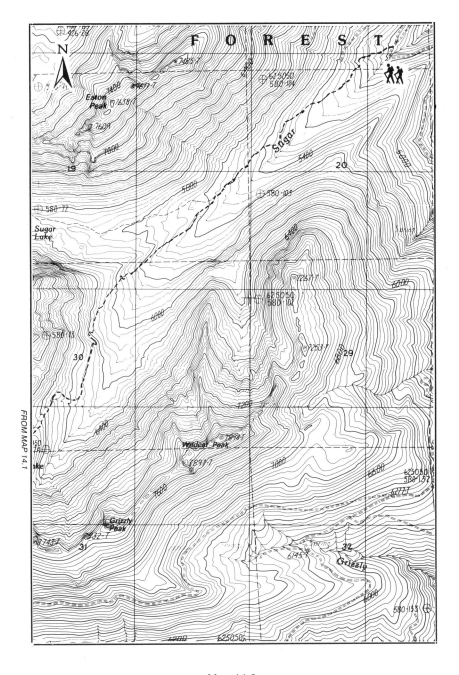

Map 14.2

15.

RUSSIAN LAKE

Destinations:	Russian Lake, Waterdog Lake, Lower Russian Lake, Golden Russian Lake, Siphon Lake.
Length:	4 miles (Deacon Lee Trail to Russian Lake)
Water:	Yes
Difficulty:	Moderate but deceptive.
Elevation:	6800 feet (trailhead)
	6600 feet (saddle)
	7100 feet (Russian Lake)
USGS 7.5" topo:	Russian Peak, Tanners Peak
	Location: T39N-R10W-Sector 8
Use intensity:	Light to moderate
Camping:	Trail Creek
Phone:	(916) 467-5757

Directions: From the south Yreka I-5 exit, follow Highway-3 through Scott Valley to Callahan. At Callahan, turn right, towards Cecilville, and head over Callahan Summit to road 39 (39N14), taking off on the right, three miles past the Trail Creek Campground turnoff. The sign at the intersection says "Russian Lake." Road 39 is steep, with numerous switchbacks and a little washboarded in spots, but wide and mostly gravel. Turnoffs are well marked, as is the trailhead. The trailhead is roomy and shaded, with parking for 20 cars along the shoulder. On the way back, be sure to turn left where the trailhead road returns to road 39. The intersection can be confusing.

❖ ❖ ❖

The Russians are coming, the Russians are coming

You'd think a trail which begins at 6800 feet and ends at 7100 feet after four miles, would be ridiculously easy. That was my reasoning when I persuaded my wife to accompany me on what I figured to be a quiet stroll though the woods to a pretty lake. While she enjoys alpine splendor as much as I, she does not share my enthusiasm for challenge and perspiration. I try to take this into account before inviting her with me.

While the route lived up to or surpassed all expectations as far as scenery, it proved puzzlingly difficult. Aside from being almost entirely in the open, with hardly any shade and 100 degree heat, it kept rising and dropping hundreds of feet for no apparent reason. They were not gentle ups and downs, either. It became extremely annoying after a while.

Still, it was quite an experience, highlighted, a mile up the path, by one of the most amazing panoramas I've seen in 24 years of hiking the region. In addition, Russian Lake, at the trail end, ranks well up on my list of "hidden gems."

From the trailhead, the path drops gently through an all too brief woods of Western white pine and red fir. Coming around a point, it emerges into a large clearcut. Eventually, the trail will make its way around the basin to the saddle on your left, then around the peak on the basin's far side, to the saddle and mountain beyond. Russian Lake lies four miles distant, just over the far saddle, on the north side of the white peak.

The first saddle, a scant mile from the trailhead, is unbelievable. Looking north, you see the entire Marble Mountain Wilderness, including the Marble Rim (Chapter 3) and the English Peak areas (Chapter 7). The canyon of the Salmon River's North Fork is easily traced.

Looking south, you're almost directly opposite the main rise of the Trinity Alps, which shoot up from the South Fork of the Salmon to over 9000 feet. Thompson Peak, highest in the Trinity Alps, forms the core of the group. It's the one with active glaciers.

I did a little research on the Thompson Peak glaciers in 1992, while writing my book on the Trinity Alps. Maps of the area show two main glaciers, each 1½ miles wide by a half-mile long, plus some smaller glaciers. Despite the fact that glaciers are extremely unstable, every published map since at least the 1950's, has shown them exactly the same. However, on a 1991 Forest Service aerial photo I obtained, the glaciers had shrunk by 90 percent, to the size of a city block.

East of Thompson Peak, look for Caribou Peak, with Deadman Peak anchoring the vista's eastern end. Long Gulch Lake, Trail Gulch Lake and Fish Lake all lurk within the immense glacial cirques gouged into Deadman Peak. The side road to Trail Creek Campground, passed on the main highway near the road 39 turnoff, accesses these trailheads. The view of Deadman Peak from the Deacon Lee Trail peers directly into the Fish Lake Cirque. Another 100 feet of elevation would enable you to see the lake.

Past the saddle, the Deacon Lee Trail slowly makes its way up a long, rocky pitch to an even rockier point. Beyond, the path continues to climb steeply, then enters the woods and abruptly drops, through a tight switchback, into a large draw. The bottom of the draw is an area of tremendous blowdown, with giant trees, broken and uprooted, scattered all over the place.

Beyond the blowdown, the trail continues through the woods, passing two small creeks dispensing the only water between trailhead and lake. The Whites Gulch Trail, taking off left near the creeks, climbs 500 feet in ¼ mile, then drops into Whites Gulch. It ends after 5½ miles, at a road near Sawyers Bar.

Immediately after the creeks, the route passes a series of upland meadows, with continuing excellent views. Then it makes its way through more level, heavily grazed meadows where a false trail veers off to the right. Stay high. Soon after, in the woods near the trail's last major pitch, the path makes the last of it's notorious drop/climbs, losing and regaining 300 feet for absolutely no reason.

When you start seeing granite boulders, you're approaching the Russian Lake junction. Turn right for Siphon Lake and the Pacific Crest Trail and left for Waterdog and Russian Lakes, less than ¼ mile away.

The final push to Waterdog Lake climbs a short but steep hill, then contours around a wooded slope high above Lower Russian Lake. Like the saddle three miles back, this short pitch offers a world class vista. The first thing you see as you come over the top, is the rocky basin of Lower Russian Lake, 500 feet below, bounded by Russian Peak on the east and an unnamed, glistening white, 7900 foot summit on the west. Yet another lake, Golden Russian, lies in a pocket on the slopes of the 7900 foot peak. There is no trail to either Lower Russian or Golden Russian Lake.

To reach Lower Russian Lake, follow the Waterdog Lake outlet on the far side. There should be a faint way trail down to the bench containing the lower lake and a small pond. Lower Russian Lake covers two acres at 6500 feet, reaches a depth of 12 feet and is home to a naturally propagating brook trout population.

Pat Bernstein, Deacon Lee Trail

Golden Russian Lake is 500 feet lower than Lower Russian Lake, in an adjacent basin to the northwest. Either scramble around the point or follow the Lower Russian outlet until it meets the Golden Russian outlet. Golden Russian Lake covers 1½ acres at 6080 feet and is eight feet deep. It was named for the Sierra Nevada golden trout some private citizens stocked it with decades ago. The fish may or may not still be there. If they are, it's the only lake in the region containing this species.

Fish Lake, in the Trinity Alps, whose cirque is prominently visible across the canyon from the Deacon Lee Trail, is the region's only lake stocked with arctic grayling.

The most prominent feature visible from the Deacon Lee Trail immediately before (and at) Waterdog Lake, is the looming western slope of Russian Peak, highest mountain in the Wilderness at 8196 feet. The slope appears as a solid gray wall, unbroken and unvarying for four miles above South Russian Creek, thousands of feet below. The PCT, gouged rudely into the wall's flank, is visible for miles.

Russian Peak's western wall reminded me of the wall rising above the Stuart Fork of the Trinity River, at Morris Meadows in the Trinity Alps, not far away. While the Morris Meadows wall was clearly carved by a giant valley glacier, the main valley below Russian Peak does not fit the profile of a glacial valley, except for small cirques at the headwaters. If not the result of a glacier, the wall is probably a fault line.

It is ¼ mile from the Siphon Lake junction to Waterdog Lake, charmingly nestled in the woods on a high bench above Lower Russian Lake. A large meadow occupies the shore on the lake's upper end. Waterdog Lake covers 3½ acres at 7000 feet elevation. The fairly popular puddle is 16 feet deep and stocked with brook and rainbow trout.

Above Waterdog Lake, you see meadows, then a forested slope, then a triangular rocky headwall. Russian Lake sits at the base of the headwall, near the top of the mountain, ⅛ mile away. To reach it, follow the main path around the lake's eastern shore, uphill and out of the basin, to the saddle between Waterdog Lake and South Russian Creek. Head up the ridge to the right, off the trail, until you meet another trail, coming up from the meadow at Waterdog Lake. My route is easier than explaining how to find the trail in the meadow.

From the high saddle, the Deacon Lee Trail descends to South Russian Creek, which it follows for four miles to a trailhead near Idlewild Campground, near the North Fork Trailhead (Chapter 7). The South Russian Creek Trail parallels the PCT, except that the PCT, on average, runs 2000 feet higher up. South Russian Creek is one of the two primary "areas of greatest botanical diversity," for which the Russian Wilderness is famous. The other is the Duck Lake basin. See Chapters 13 and 14.

Russian Lake may be the most beautiful in the Russian Wilderness. Were it a little bigger, it would give Deep Lake, in the Marbles (Chapter 4), a run for its money as the prettiest in this book. Russian Lake is a spectacularly clear, five acre pool perched on a mountaintop and surrounded by a stunted, treeline forest of lodgepole pine, mountain hemlock, etc. The bouldery shore, clear water and white sand bottom brings to mind a giant swimming pool, which happens to be 72 feet deep. This makes it the second deepest in the Russian Wilderness, after Big Blue Lake (Chapter 11). Russian Lake sits at an elevation of 7100 feet and contains rainbow trout. *To Siphon 2 miles Some what steep —

Siphon Lake and other routes to Russian Lake

First of all, let's make one thing clear. No route to Russian Lake is superior to the Deacon Lee Trail. The Trail Creek Trail hits the lake in about the same distance, via Siphon Lake, but begins at 5100 feet instead of 6800 feet. To reach it, look for a turnoff north, uphill, a few hundred feet east of the turnoff to Trail Creek Campground, on the main highway from Callahan.

The PCT from Callahan Summit reaches Russian Lake in six miles, also via Siphon Lake. It begins at an elevation of 6200 feet.

Finally, some maps show a tempting, 2½ mile route from Jackson Lake (Chapter 14), past Siphon Lake to Russian Lake, of which two miles is closed road. Be advised that the turnoff to Jackson Lake, via road 41N16 off the Callahan-Cecilville Road, is gated, full of "No Trespassing" signs, and does not go through. I'm told the residents of the private property at Jackson Lake are quite serious about turning back trespassers.

I recommend the side trip to Siphon Lake, from the Deacon Lee Trail. It's an easy, nearly level, one mile trek from the junction just before Waterdog Lake. The route contours around the backside of the barren outcropping above Russian Lake. After heading south for ¾ mile, it meets an old, closed road, which it follows east for the last ¼ mile. Siphon Lake is a tiny, wooded pond at the base of a rocky slope. The 1½ acre, 7250 foot high pool, is 22 feet deep and stocked with rainbow trout. It gets its name from the ditch near its outlet, which siphoned water to a gold mine on the creek below.

If you continue past Siphon Lake, you'll hit the PCT in another half-mile (Chapter 16). Head south (right) for Callahan summit. Go north (left), for the Bingham Lake outlet (Chapter 14), the western wall of Russian Peak, Paynes Lake and Etna Summit.

Finally, I don't suppose anyone wants to hear about my flat tire at the Deacon Lee trailhead? The problem was, my spare was also ⅔'s flat. I inched down the interminable, bumpy, winding access road, knowing that even after I hit pavement, it was 35 miles over a high pass, to the nearest gas station...which may not even be opened.

To make a long story short, I scrounged a can of aerosol tire inflater from a kid at the Trail Creek Campground. God bless him and his offspring to the tenth generation. When I arrived at the gas station, my tire pressure was 40 pounds. I'll never leave home without aerosol tire inflater again.

Waterlog Lake

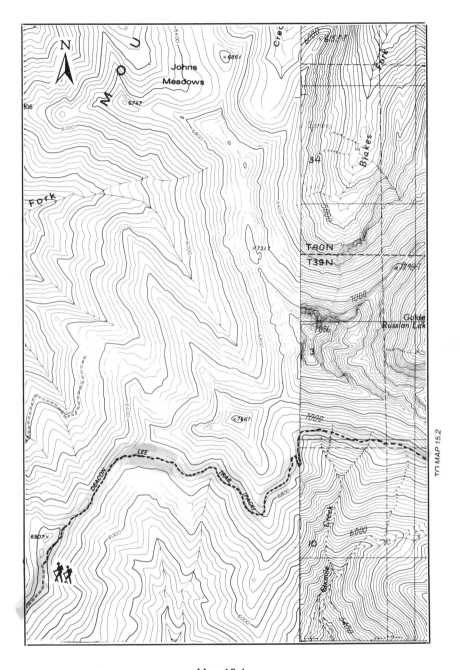

Map 15.1

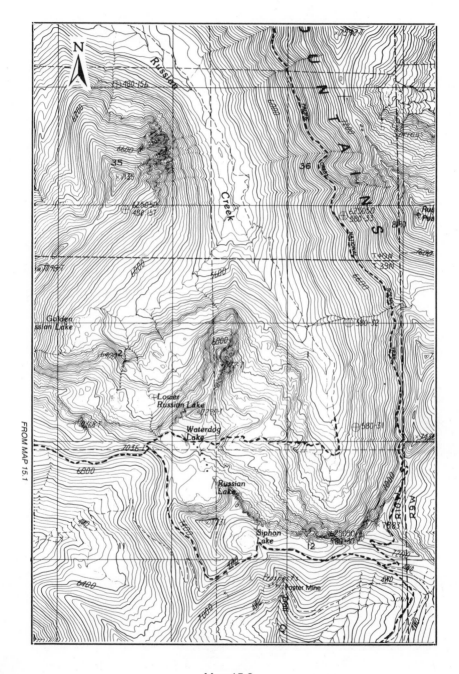

Map 15.2

16. Pacific Crest Trail/Callahan Summit to Etna Summit

Destinations:	Russian Wilderness, Bingham Lake, Statue Lake, Paynes Lake, Smith Lake, Ruffey Lakes, Meeks Meadow Lake.
Distance from Callahan summit:	5 miles (S. Wilderness boundary)
	✳ 6½ miles (Bingham Lake outlet)
	14 miles (Paynes Lake)
	15 miles (N. Wilderness boundary)
	18 miles (Ruffey Lakes)
	20 miles (Etna Summit)
Difficulty:	Easy to moderate
Elevation:	6400 feet (Callahan Summit)
	7300 feet (S. Wilderness boundary)
	7100 feet (Russian Peak traverse)
	6500 feet (Paynes Lake)
	6600 feet (N. wilderness boundary)
	7200 feet (Crest above Smith Lake)
	5900 feet (Etna Summit)
Season:	June through October
Location:	Callahan Summit - T39N-R9W-Sector 21
	Etna summit - T41N-R10W-Sector 21
Water:	Eventually
USGS 7.5" topo:	Russian Peak
Phone:	1-916-468-5351
Camping:	Carter Meadows, Idlewild
Use intensity:	Light

Directions: Callahan Summit. Leave I-5 at the south Yreka, Highway-3 exit. Take Highway-3 to Callahan and turn right onto the

Cecilville/ Forks of Salmon Road. Follow the paved road to the summit. Take the first dirt road right, just over the summit, beyond the southbound PCT parking area on the left. It leads to a small parking area for the northbound PCT into the Russian Wilderness. Callahan Summit is shown as "Carter Meadows Summit" on maps but few locals call it that.

Etna Summit. From I-5, take the south Yreka exit and follow Highway-3 to the town of Etna. Turn right on Main Street towards Sawyer's Bar and proceed up the winding, mostly paved road to the summit. Park in the well developed parking area, which holds 30 cars. Head south for the Russian Wilderness.

Through the Russians, missing everything in sight

While the Pacific Crest Trail offers a world class tour of the Marble Mountains (Chapter 10), it is not the best way to see the Russian Mountains, even though it runs right smack up the middle of the Wilderness Area's longest direction. Most of the route is confined to the long, monotonous and controversial traverse of Russian Peak. The only real highlight comes at Paynes Lake.

The most compelling reason to hike this section of the PCT would be if you're on your way up from Mexico or down from Canada. Not that the route is hideous or anything. It's beautiful. It just isn't the most advantageous trail from which to tour the Russians.

From the Callahan Summit parking area, the trail forms a giant on-ramp up a series of ever higher glacial ridges, to the central mass of the Russian Mountains. For the first mile, it climbs a rocky south slope, hitting a crest and levelling off above Little Jackson Lake, Lees Meadow and Jackson Creek. It follows the crest for the next two miles.

Views are terrific, with glacial cirque upon glacial cirque everywhere you look and white granite juxtaposed against red serpentine juxtaposed against brown metavolcanics. The largest cirques are the Trail Gulch and Long Gulch canyons, in the Trinity Alps to the south. Also to the south, you'll catch glimpses of Thompson Peak, the 9002 summit which is the highest in the Trinity Alps. It is identified by two small, active glaciers near the summit.

Before entering the Russian Wilderness, the PCT leaves the ridge, drops through a forested stand, then climbs steeply up a rock face. During the rock face climb, it meets a couple of closed roads/trails. The roads access some gold mines and begin on the section of private land around Jackson Lake.

Two side trails come in here. First, the Trail Creek Trail enters stage left. Its other end lies across the road from the turnoff to Trail Creek Campground, a few miles past Callahan Summit. The Trail Creek route gets you from the road to where you're standing two miles sooner than the PCT, but its trailhead is 1200 feet lower.

Shortly after the Trail Creek junction, the path to Siphon Lake breaks off left. This is an outstanding little trip. It's a nearly level ¾ mile to tiny Siphon Lake and another level mile to Waterdog Lake. Russian Lake (Chapter 15), a deep, clear, five acre pool which may be the prettiest in the Wilderness, lies on a bench ⅛ mile above Waterdog Lake. These are the last easily accessed lakes until Paynes Lake, many miles north. The view of Russian Peak, with the PCT rudely gouged into its eastern lank, is outstanding from Waterdog Lake.

Beyond the Siphon Lake junction, the PCT switches up a steep hill, then swings briefly onto the crest above Jackson Lake, a 28 acre gem on private property, from which all access is barred (They can't stop us from looking, though).

A short contour above Jackson Lake, and a short climb over the crest, leads to the Wilderness boundary and the South Russian Creek drainage. The next four miles have been blasted into the gray, mostly treeless western wall of Russian Peak. As noted, there was some controversy over the routing of the PCT here because it is visible for miles and doesn't exactly blend in with the landscape. While I can understanding avoiding the top of Russian Peak, it might have been better to run the trail past High Lake and Little Duck Lake. The present route high is bouldery, brushy, boring and barren.

A mile into the Wilderness, the trail crosses the Bingham Lake outlet creek. Bingham Lake (Chapter 14) covers 12 acres in a steep walled cirque at the foot of Russian Peak, less than ¼ mile above the trail. It's well worth a look, despite the difficult, bouldery climb. You'd do better to begin contouring up before reaching the outlet creek. If you have a hankering to climb 8196 foot Russian Peak, begin at Bingham Lake.

The traverse of the Russian Peak wall ends, mercifully, just past a jagged spire called "the Statue." Soon after, the trail crosses the ridge and swings northeast into the woods, away from South Russian Creek. If you climb up the ridge for ¼ mile, instead of staying on the trail, you'll reach Statue Lake, a picturesque, one acre, 15 foot deep pond at 7200 feet, stocked with brook trout.

The next two miles are uneventful as the path wanders through the woods, holding its 6800 foot contour. Expect lingering snow on these north facing, forested slopes. The trail eventually works its way to a wooded saddle, crossing the Horse Range Trail which leads east to Lipstick Lake and the Duck Lake trailhead. If you go west here, you'll hit the South Russian Creek road system in a half-mile. It's six miles by trail and road from the Horse Range junction to Sawyers Bar, on the North Fork of the Salmon.

Beyond the junction, the PCT climbs briefly, making its way around the headwall above minuscule Lipstick Lake (Chapter 13). After that, its a pretty much level, 1½ miles to Paynes Lake, highlight of the trip.

If you've ever hiked the Paynes Lake Trail (Chapter 12), you'll be grateful for the reasonably level, scenic approach afforded by the PCT. The Paynes Lake Trail climbs 2000 feet in 2½ miles to the popular, 17 acre lake set in a wide, meadowy basin. A side trail around Paynes Lake leads to Albers Lake in a half-mile.

A last day-hike: Smith Lake

The final 3½ mile PCT trek, from Paynes Lake to Etna Summit, mostly outside the Wilderness, ranks among this book's more worthwhile and easy day-hikes. So nice, in fact, that I have reversed directions for this last segment, beginning at Etna Summit. Etna Summit itself offers one of California's more impressive vistas, with the Marble Mountains on one side, the Russians on the other, and the deep green chasm of the Salmon River dropping down thousands of feet and several miles to an infinite western horizon.

From the Etna Summit trailhead (with parking for 10 cars), the path grows ever more spectacular as it slowly gains elevation and the Marble and Russians come increasingly into view. Most of the Marbles eventually make an appearance, except for the Marble Rim. Look for English Peak and a brief glimpse of Salmon Mountain, in the Trinity Alps, far to the west. In the Russians, you can see improving views of the sheer, rocky cirques of Taylor Lake, Hogan Lake and Big Blue Lake. The PCT's initial 1½ miles cuts an absolutely straight swath at a slightly uncomfortable uphill gradient that never varies. A switchback shown on the Forest Service map near the trailhead does not exist.

After 1½ miles and a rise of 900 feet, the PCT intersects the upper end of the road which runs from the Taylor Lake trailhead to the Ruffey Lake trailhead. You're probably better off using the PCT to reach this spot, although a high clearance 4x4 or an ATV could make it. From the crossing, it's several hundred very steep, uphill feet to the road end at the ridgetop, with parking for four cars. From the road end, hike along the ridge 100 feet for a view of Ruffey Lake, a yuck brown, 2½ acre pool in a dense woods, at 6400 feet. The lake is eight feet deep and stocked with brook trout. Ruffey Lake offers the best camping between Paynes Lake and several miles beyond Etna Summit. A ¼ mile trail leads down to Ruffey Lake from the ridgetop. There are also a couple ponds called Lower Ruffey Lake and Meeks Meadow Lake in the vicinity, both stocked with brook trout.

From the Ruffey Lake/PCT junction, the PCT crosses a couple of wet meadows, then hits the ridge above Meeks Meadow. While views are magnificent, they don't compare to the panorama from Smith Lake, a mile up the trail. Look for a beautiful stand of windswept mountain mahogany just before the Smith Lake basin. This is a very diverse botanical area, with oceanspray, serviceberry, chokecherry and bittercherry in addition to mountain mahogany.

Exquisite and surprising, Smith Lake bears no resemblance to Ruffey Lake. Smith's intense, emerald green, six acre pool has little shoreline vegetation and sits at the base of a nearly perpendicular, white granite cliff. The PCT is quite precarious here as it makes its way across the rock face, several hundred feet above the water. Horses should be led through this section as the trail becomes a stone staircase in a couple places. The short climb down to the lake is easier than it looks, however, although once there, there are precious few level campsites, if any.

One of the area's deeper lakes at 56 feet, Smith is stocked with brook, rainbow and brown trout. A log fallen into the water near the western shore is nearly straight up and down. East of the lake, most of Scott

Valley can be seen, with the Duzel Rock range rising beyond and Mount Shasta beyond that.

Immediately beyond the Smith Lake cirque, the PCT drops into a wide basin, beginning with a couple short switchbacks. From the first switchback, a low, "V" notch can be seen, $\frac{1}{4}$ mile away, with the upper end of the Taylor Lake cirque visible on the other side. The PCT hits the notch briefly, revealing 12 acre Taylor Lake (Chapter 11), less than $\frac{1}{2}$ mile away. A very steep scramble trail leads down to the lake.

Pacific Crest Trail above Smith Lake

Beyond the notch, the PCT sidehills along a steep mountainside for a mile. It then swings in and out of a narrow canyon, crosses the Wilderness boundary and meets the lower end of Paynes Lake, two miles from Smith Lake.

And that, dear friends, is absolutely everything there is to be said about the Marble Mountain and Russian Wilderness Areas.

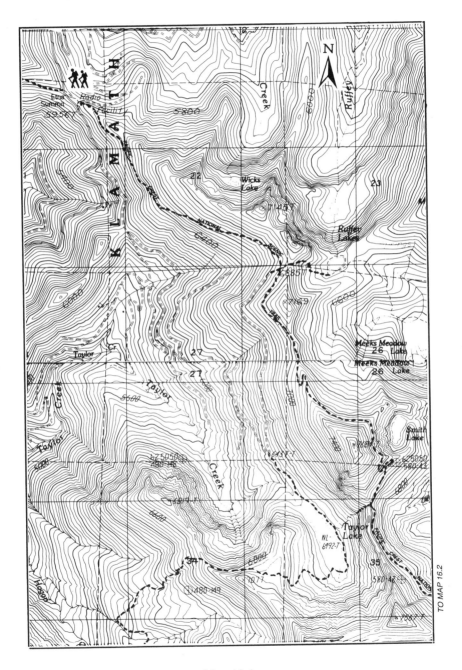

Map 16.1

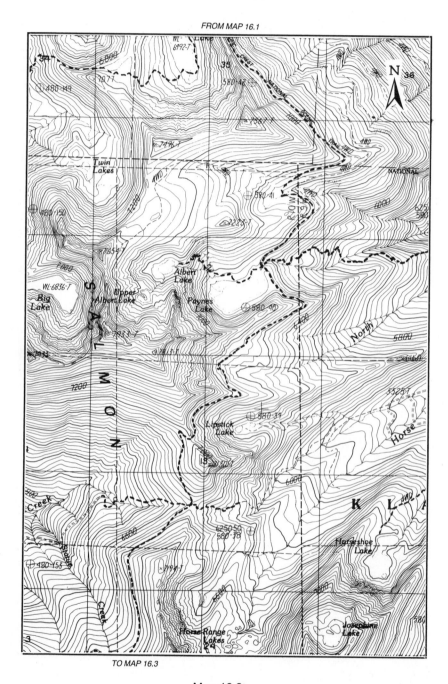

Map 16.2

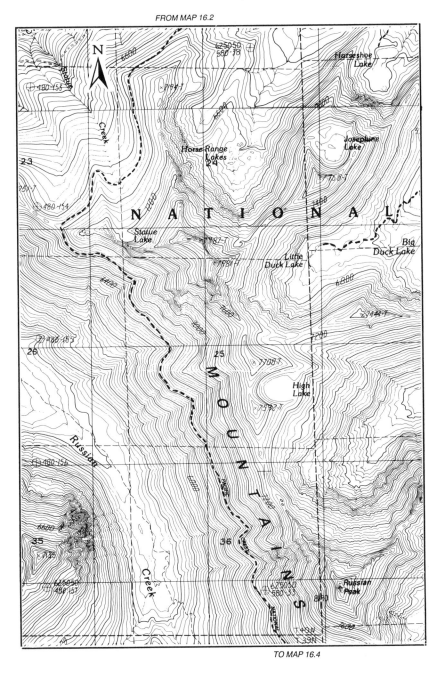

FROM MAP 16.2

Map 16.3

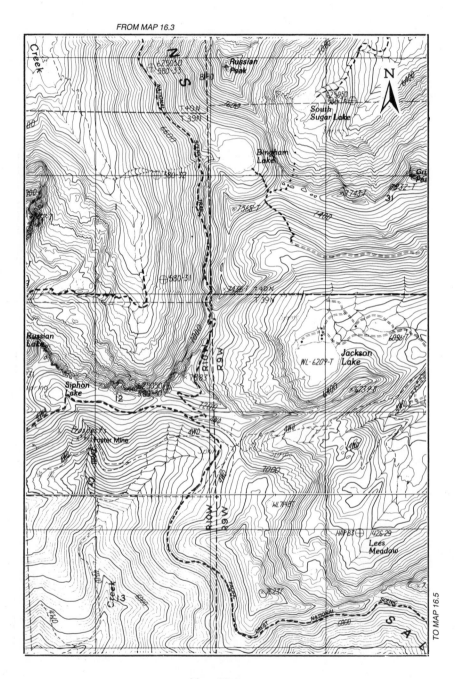

Map 16.4

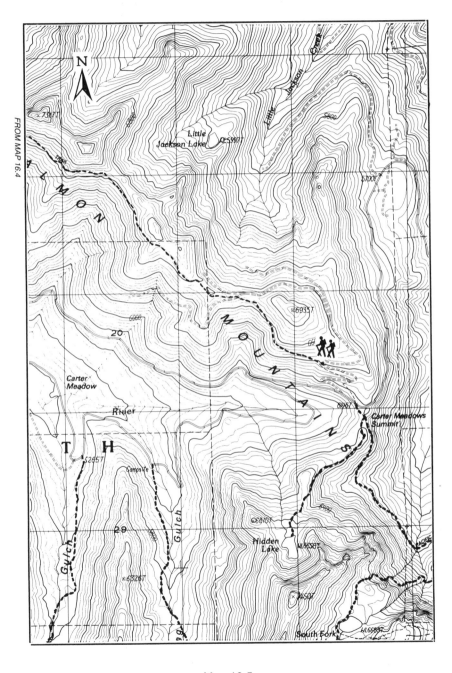

Map 16.5

Best Hikes of the
MARBLE MOUNTAIN
and Russian Wilderness Areas
California

Destinations Index

OTHER MOUNTAIN N'AIR BOOKS

Backpacking Primer
Lori Saldaña
ISBN: 1-879415-13-5 $12.00

Best Day Hikes of the California Northwest
Art Bernstein
ISBN: 1-879415-02-X $13.50

Best Hikes of the Trinity Alps
Art Bernstein
ISBN: 1-879415-05-4 $17.00

Portland Hikes
Art Benstein, and Andrew Jackman
ISBN: 1-879415-09-7 $18.00

Cross Country-NORTHEAST
John R. Fitzgerald Jr.
ISBN: 1-879415-07-0 $12.00

Cross Country Skiing in Southern California
Eugene Mezereny
ISBN: 1-879415-08-9 $14.00

Great Rock Hits of Hueco Tanks
Paul Piana
ISBN: 1-879415-03-8 $6.95

Mountain Bike Adventures... MOAB, Utah
Bob Ward
ISBN: 1-879415-11-9 $15.00

The Rogue River Guide
Kevin Keith Tice
ISBN: 1-879415-12-7 $15.00

High Endeavors
Pat Ament
ISBN: 1-879415-00-3 $12.95

A Night On The Ground A Day In The Open
Doug Robinson
ISBN: 1-879415-14-3 $19.00

On Mountains & Mountaineers
Mikel Vause
ISBN: 1-879415-06-2 $12.95

Rock and Roses
Mikel Vause, editor
ISBN: 1-879415-01-1 $11.95

Cooking With Strawberries
Margaret and Virginia Clark
ISBN: 1-879415-26-7 $10.95

SALADS A to Z
Margaret and Virginia Clark
ISBN: 1-879415-25-9 $13.00

All Mountain N' Air Books are generally available at most bookstores and outdoor equipment retail outlets. They are also available at local libraries. If your favorite store or library does not carry them or out of stock, ask them to special order any of these books from **Mountain N' Air Books**, P.O. Box 12540, La Crescenta, CA 91224 or call 800-446-9696.

* 2 people
Tent 2-Pads
Sleeping Bag
Zip Lock Bages

-get By-
-Nice To have-

5 days - 2 shirts
2 under wear
2 socks
1 long pants
1 short pants
1 sweat shirt
1 Rain Poncho
1 Boots 1 tennies

Notes:

* Water Dog Fresh water
pipe in hill side
4-5 camp sites

* 2 Black plastic
Bages for packs
at night.

* 4 to 5 camp site at
Russian Lake

? Fishing gear

* 1 Base camp- day hicks
from Base camp.

* Coffie pot / Coffee
\ Hot coco

* Frieing Pan + Foil
* pate - were
* S o S pads

air matress?

- Food -

* Rice A Roni - Butter   French Bread
mc + cheese   Ham + cheese
Becon - Hot Cakes - Syrup chips

Dryed Fruit   Jerkey

* Tang? Dryed Drinks
mix with water

* ch. Bars - Snacks

- Pills - !!

* First aid - ace Bandage
Sun Screen?   Roll guse pad
               Band aids
               Baby Wipes

maggito Repelent
aniceptic Pads
Tape - Soap Tooth past
Shampoo + Powder Brushes
B.o. Stick

* maps - Two of area !

*
Dog Food, Tie out
Leash, muzzle,

* aug 1998 - Snow for Ice packs